the series on school reform

Patricia A. Wasley
University of Washington

Ann Lieberman
Carnegie Foundation for the
Advancement of Teaching

Joseph P. McDonald
New York University

SERIES EDITORS

(Continued)

the series on school reform, *continued*

Building
School-Based
Teacher Learning
Communities

Professional Strategies to
Improve Student Achievement

Milbrey W. McLaughlin
Joan E. Talbert

Teachers College
Columbia University
New York and London

Published by Teachers College Press, 1234 Amsterdam Avenue, New York, NY 10027

Library of Congress Cataloging-in-Publication Data

McLaughlin, Milbrey W.
    Building school-based teacher learning communities : professional strategies to improve student achievement / Milbrey W. McLaughlin, Joan E. Talbert.
      p. cm. — (the series on school reform)
    Includes bibliographical references and index.
    ISBN-13: 978-0-8077-4680-6 (cloth : alk. paper)
    ISBN-13: 978-0-8077-4679-0 (pbk. : alk. paper)
    1. Teachers — Training of — United States. 2. Teachers — In-service training — United States. 3. Educational change — United States. I. Talbert, Joan E. II. Title. III. the series on school reform (New York, N.Y.)

LB1715.M348 2006
370.71'55—dc22

                                                 2005055956

ISBN-13:   ISBN-10:
978-0-8077-4679-0 (paper)   0-8077-4679-7 (paper)
978-0-8077-4680-6 (cloth)   0-8077-4680-0 (cloth)

Printed on acid-free paper

Manufactured in the United States of America

13 12 11 10 09 08 07   8 7 6 5 4 3

Contents

Acknowledgments

We learned about the character, consequences, and development of school-based teacher learning communities from the more than 15 years of research on education reform carried out by Stanford's Center for Research on the Context of Teaching (CRC). Our debt to the many researchers and practitioners who participated in various CRC efforts extends across several projects involving many schools and districts. A National Science Foundation study involved us with innovative mathematics departments. Evaluations of two major education reform initiatives, the Students at the Center (SATC) project, funded by the DeWitt Wallace–Reader's Digest Fund, and the Bay Area School Reform Collaborative (BASRC), supported primarily by grants from the Annenberg and Hewlett foundations, brought us into sustained contact with school-level reform efforts and their diverse contexts. A research project undertaken in partnership with colleagues at the federally supported Center for the Study of Teaching and Policy (CTP) at the University of Washington focused on district reform in several states. The education reform initiatives we studied offered opportunities to understand the problems and processes of building effective school communities; our documentation of these efforts forms the book's evidence base.

The Students at the Center initiative, carried out in Chicago, New York, and Philadelphia from 1996 to 2001, funded several professional development organizations in each city to collaborate to improve teaching quality in district schools. Our CRC research team involved graduate students and research staff in field-based research and qualitative and quantitative analyses over the 5 years of the initiative. Stacey Pelika played the pivotal role of SATC project director and made major contributions to the project's data analysis and reporting. Stacey's black-belt organizing skills kept years of interview and record data accessible, and her terrific recall made her indispensable to team members seeking to retrieve an interview or make connections across sites. Although this book has changed significantly from its original conception and drafting, we are grateful to Stacey for her key role in developing some of the case analyses that we draw upon here. Teresa McCaffrey joined the project staff during the last phase of data collection and analysis; she took the lead in analyzing the Chicago SATC parent project featured in chapter 6. Stanford School of Education doctoral students formed the core research team and brought particular analytic lenses and contributions to understanding implementation challenges and outcomes of the SATC design. Linda Friedrich was lead researcher for the New York SATC site, and her dissertation analyzed collaboration among the initiative's professional developers there. Patricia Burch headed up the Chicago SATC research; her dissertation examined how "marginal" community-based organizations such as the arts interact with "mainstream" education organizations. Chapter 6's discussion of the Chicago art project's success with community engagement and political diplomacy draws upon her research. Cynthia Coburn and Ellen Meyer were key field researchers in Philadelphia and Chicago, respectively. Ginger Cook and Kim Powell contributed to the last phase of field research in New York City and Philadelphia, respectively, and participated in the initial data analysis and writing.

Phase 1 of the Bay Area School Reform Collaborative took place from 1996 to 2001 and featured inquiry processes throughout a school as a vehicle for developing teacher learning communities capable of improving student learning and closing achievement gaps. The CRC evaluation involved a team of researchers in 10 case study schools; repeated surveys of 86 Leadership Schools; and observation of many workshops, institutes, staff meetings, network convenings and other BASRC regional sessions. BASRC project researchers contributing to the evidence base cited here include Betty Achinstein, Mike Copland, Becky Crowe, Rachel Ebby, Jennifer Goldstein, Jim Greeno, Ed Haertel, Ken Ikeda, Julia Imburg, Anastasia Karaglani, Wendy Lin, Jacob Mishook, Kay Moffitt, Ida Oberman, Laura Post, Marjorie Wechsler, Catherine Roller White, and Joel Zarrow. Dana Mitra took the lead in analyzing stages of BASRC schools' development of inquiry processes and teacher learning communities, described in chapter 2. Celine Toomey Coggins's dissertation on coaching during BASRC's second phase (2001–2005) focused on the two BASRC schools and districts featured in chapters 3 and 4. A study of math education reform in a satellite sample of California high schools complemented findings from the BASRC evaluation. In particular, Joanne Lieberman's dissertation research, sponsored by the National Science Foundation, focused on the mathematics department featured in chapter 2.

Our research on reforming districts supported by CTP also contributed to this book's empirical base. CTP's research program studied reform strategies and practices at the state, district, and school levels in California, New York, North Carolina, and Washington; the work of the entire CTP team, led by Michael Knapp at the University of Washington, informed our analyses of district contexts. Case studies of district reform efforts developed by Amy Hightower and Julie Marsh provide foundation for chapters 5 and 6.

Practice grounds this book's argument and evidence. The teachers, administrators, professional developers, and teacher community facilitators who opened their professional lives to our research teams helped us to understand the principles that guide their work with teacher communities, the ways in which local contexts matter to them, the challenges and successes they experience, and the conditions that support their learning and effectiveness.

The Students at the Center initiative included professional developers and consultants from diverse organizations in each city. In Chicago, the SATC effort involved Smokey Daniels, director of the Illinois Writing Project, and colleagues at the Center for City Schools at National-Louis University, including Angelee Johns, Linda Bailey, Lynette Emmons, and Peter Leki, who coordinated the Parent Project; Cleeta Ryals, acting director of the Chicago Algebra Project, and consultant Imara Randall; Arnold April, executive director of the Chicago Arts Partnership in Education, and his colleagues; and Allen Swartz, executive director of the Chicago Metro-History Education Center, and colleague Lisa Oppenheim. Judith Foster and Litrea Hunter of Chicago Public Schools' Teachers' Academy for Professional Growth and principals and teachers in four anonymous case study schools provided generous insight into how SATC looked to them and what it accomplished in their schools.

New York's SATC project team involved Rick Lear and Anthony Conelli, who successively served as SATC project directors over the five-year period. Many consultants from the Lehman College Institute for Literacy Studies and its director, Marcie Wolfe, were involved in the team. They included Ray Durney, director of the New York City Math Project, and NYCMP consultant Linda Dolinko, whose work with a middle school is featured in chapters 3 and 4; Linette Moorman, director of the New York City Writing Project, and consultants Ed Osterman and Alan Stein; Elaine Avidon, director of the Elementary Teachers Network, whose work with a middle school is featured in chapter 3, and ETN co-director Barbara Batton; Brett Eynon, education director of the American Social History Project at Hunter College and consultant Eliza Fabrillar; Hubert Dyasi, director of the City College Science Workshop Center, and consultant Mitch Bleier; Steve Goodman, executive director of the Education Video Center, and consultants Jeremy Engle, Amy Melnick, and Betsy Newman; Lucy Calkins, director of the Teachers College Reading and Writing Project, and associate director Laurie Pessah; and Keith Hefner, director of Youth Communications, Inc. and colleague Sean Chambers. Practitioners associated with New York SATC gave liberally of their time and perspective. Margaret Harrington, executive director for School Programs and Support Services of the Board of Education of the City of New York and Elayna Konstan, director of instruction for alternative high schools, provided invaluable perspective on the project and its contexts. Principals and teachers of four anonymous case study schools were critical collaborators both in our field research and efforts to make sense of what we saw and heard in their schools.

In Philadelphia, SATC staff and consultants included project director Deborah Jumpp; Judy Buchanan, Betsy Useem, and Nancy McGinley (director) of the Philadelphia Education Fund; Marci Resnick, director of the Philadelphia Writing Project, and consultant Michele Bell; Molly McLaughlin, director of teacher education at The Franklin Institute, and museum educator Susan Holmes; and Deborah Pomeroy, Coordinator of Science Education at Beaver College, and colleague Anna May Davidson. Philadelphia administrators responsible for the district's cluster school arrangement played a key role in developing our knowledge of the district and community and our appreciation of the special challenges reformers faced there. Teachers and administrators at our four anonymous case study schools likewise were openhanded in their welcome to our researchers and invitation into their schools.

The many professionals involved with the Bay Area School Reform Collaborative have been invaluable guides, interpreters, and respondents as they worked to develop BASRC's work over its first 5 years and as we sought to document its theory of action and consequences for participating schools and districts. BASRC intermediary leaders helped us to understand their theory of action and approaches to building capacity of reform coordinators and leaders in schools and districts to build communities of practice for continual school improvement. Most notable among these BASRC leaders are Merrill Vargo, executive director since

1995; Pam Stoddard, research director, and her successor, Ida Oberman; Rick Damellio and Carlene Gundersgaard, who headed the district reform work beginning in 2001, and their successor, Jim Brown; and former superintendents who coached BASRC districts during this period, including Walt Buster, Marcia Plumleigh, and Sharon Robinson. Reform leaders in participating schools and districts were key sources of information about the implementation of BASRC's theory of action. We are especially grateful to Leni von Blanckensee, BASRC reform coordinator in Alameda, whose work with a Bay Area middle school is featured in chapter 3. Other reform coordinators and support providers whose work in and with the anonymous case study schools we followed over the years helped us understand concretely their essential role in fostering teacher learning communities. Principals and teachers in these case study schools unfailingly welcomed our research team and made time in their crowded days to speak with us about their work.

Administrators, consultants, teachers, and community members involved in CTP research in reforming districts likewise gave of scarce time, opened their schools and records to us, and participated in candid conversations about the strengths and shortfalls of their district reform efforts, lessons learned, and the district role in school and instructional reform. Three of our case study districts and the educators associated with them are anonymous; San Diego City Schools is the exception. In San Diego, we were fortunate to enter the district simultaneously with Anthony Alvarado, the chancellor for instruction and designer of the district's Blueprint for Reform. Alvarado's, Superintendent Alan Bersin's, and standards and assessment director Karen Bachofer's frank assessments of the district's efforts were invaluable. Other San Diego district administrators were similarly forthcoming and provided us a comprehensive understanding of reform from the district perspective, from budgets to human relations to instructional support. Principals and teachers in our anonymous San Diego case study schools enabled us to see how Blueprint strategies and supports played out in their settings.

CRC staff provided the complex organization and supports essential to multifaceted, multisite field-based projects. Barbara Rogers handled the flood of tapes for transcription, never lost one, and all the while maintained the cordial relationships with our far-flung transcribers that enabled occasional requests for urgent attention. Julie Cummer, Nancy McCaa, and Susan Watkins kept complicated project accounts and expenditures on the up-and-up; Barbara and Susan assisted with preparation of the final manuscript.

All of these talented researchers and professionals contributed to the research and practice-based understandings that ground this book on school-based teacher learning communities. Credit for the idea and support for the book goes to Edward Pauley, evaluation director at the DeWitt Wallace-Reader's Digest Funds (currently Wallace Fund). He, along with Adam Stoll, our program officer, believed that a book bringing together evidence from diverse CRC research projects, as well as other relevant literature and experience, would be of greater value to the field than would the scheduled final report to the Funds on the Students at the Center initiative. Ed has been a generous and patient colleague as we drafted and redrafted the prospectus and several versions of this book. He, along with Carla Asher, the Funds' program officer who devised the SATC initiative; colleagues Edwin Bridges, Linda Friedrich, Ann Lieberman, and Joseph McDonald; and two anonymous reviewers provided valuable feedback on manuscript drafts, and we hope the book reflects their good advice. Cynthia Haven's superb editorial skills rooted out jargon and challenged opaque constructions—though some no doubt remain.

Work on this book provided a rare opportunity to reflect across almost two decades of CRC research and to pull together evidence across multiple national initiatives regarding challenges and prospects for significantly improving urban public education. We hope the result makes the contribution Ed Pauley anticipated and that it captures the wisdom of the extraordinary learning community that has developed around our research over the years. Thank you all.

1

Learning to Improve Student Achievement

Two pressures fuel today's urgency about teachers' learning opportunities. First, our society demands schools that produce students with the complex intellectual skills that are needed by the "knowledge society," but missing in too many of their graduates. Second, we can no longer accept the unequal student outcomes that have characterized American schools for generations, with advantaged students achieving more academically than students with fewer resources to support their learning. This inequity has directed more attention to teachers' knowledge, skills, and norms of practice. From the federal government to states and districts, the call is for all children to learn to high standards and to have access to high-quality instruction. Advances in cognitive science and learning theory make clearer what meeting this challenge entails. We know a great deal more about how students learn, and those principles for learning depart radically from the behaviorist routines and teacher-directed roles seen in most classrooms (Donovan & Bransford, 2005).

Pressures to change and improve the nation's schools spotlight teachers' capability to provide the kinds of classroom experiences needed to improve all students' learning and achievement. They require forms of instruction and pedagogy that are foreign to many teachers, as well as a fundamental reconceptualization of learning. Not enough teachers can organize instruction to highlight the cognitive skills that our new knowledge society expects. Not enough teachers can work successfully with students from diverse cultural, ethnic, and economic backgrounds. Not enough teachers can relinquish the role of classroom "sage" and knowledge transmitter to assume a new role focused on facilitating problem-solving and developing knowledge among students. The challenges posed for American education require substantial teacher learning resources.

Policymakers and reformers have addressed these pressures with a disparate array of efforts to improve teachers' instructional skills and students' learning. Some are tied to such instructional programs as "Success for All," or to adopting specific curriculums offered by, for example, Open Court or Houghton Mifflin. These efforts attempt to train teachers in prescribed activities, and ask them to implement project strategies faithfully. Others, linked with state or local gap-closing efforts, require teachers' professional development aimed at bringing up the bottom of student achievement distribution; they revamp classroom practices to help traditionally underachieving students. Still other professional development resources try to boost instruction in areas viewed as critical to America's economic success, most particularly mathematics and science.

This book accepts society's sober assessment about the limited and unequal capability of America's teachers to meet the educational needs of all students. It also acknowledges the consequent need for teachers to develop new forms of teaching and strategies to meet the needs of a diverse, continually changing student population. Teachers must make more than technical changes in their practices, however, to provide the learning environments and student outcomes society demands. Effective schools and classrooms also require teacher professionalism that embraces new norms and expectations for students' learning. Its service ethic will guide relations with students and colleagues. Its hallmark will be a commitment to lifelong professional learning and collective responsibility for improved student learning. Because it requires cultural change, this fundamental and critical alteration in teachers' work and workplace is more difficult to accomplish than technical modification in practice.

The argument for school-based teacher learning communities motivates this book. This position reflects the necessary limits of externally defined and delivered professional development resources, and the kind of learning and change asked of teachers. External learning resources such as workshops associated with special projects or "in-service" sessions tied to new curricula typically represent others' ideas about needed skills and knowledge but seldom reflect teachers' thoughts about what they need to learn or how to learn it. Curriculum developers, state policymakers, or various "education experts" decide what and how teachers should learn. These externally developed professional development opportunities almost never build on teachers' knowledge or day-to-day classroom challenges.

Experience teaches that externally driven professional development efforts are likely to be episodic in their consequences for practice or education reform. They tend to be pasted onto existing instructional and institutional arrangements, with little attention to issues of sustaining improvement or deepening practice (Tyack & Cuban, 1996). History also shows that externally driven reforms and the teacher development resources that accompany them can promote incoherence in both school and district instructional offerings when they derive from different instructional philosophies, use diverse and not always compatible instructional materials, or in other ways represent different approaches to teachers' classroom work (Newmann & Associates, 1996). Pundits coined the term "Christmas tree" to represent the many unconnected special projects or fashionable reforms adopted by schools and districts in response to attractive funding opportunities. Other observers of the local school reform scene labeled this tendency to amass short-term and unrelated initiatives as "projectitis," signaling the superficial and ephemeral quality of imported initiatives.

A more fundamental issue limits the effectiveness of externally driven professional development efforts, however. Even the highest-quality professional development resources will falter unless teachers can work together on new ideas and reflect on practice and its implications for students' learning. These external knowledge resources can be vital ingredients to improve student learning, but they cannot be enough to meet society's goals without opportunities for teachers to situate them in their own classrooms or school contexts. Moreover, they are not enough to develop professionalism in teaching and accountability for all students' learning. These goals require change in professional culture grounded in teachers' active involvement in a school-based learning community (Louis & Marks, 1998; McLaughlin & Talbert, 2002). Improved student learning depends upon teacher learning; however, we argue that the ultimate payoff of teachers' learning opportunities depends upon teachers' opportunities and commitment to work together to improve instruction for the students in their school.

THE ESSENTIAL ROLE OF A SCHOOL-BASED LEARNING COMMUNITY FOR TEACHERS

Various definitions of "teacher learning community" exist, but they all feature a common image of a professional community where teachers work collaboratively to reflect on their practice, examine evidence about the relationship between practice and student outcomes, and make changes that improve teaching and learning for the particular students in their classes. Temporary off-site teacher learning communities thrive in various locations. The National Writing Project is perhaps the best known network of teacher learners and a valued resource for teachers and school-based learning communities across the country (Lieberman & Wood, 2003). The Writers' Workshops also are popular with practitioners. Breadloaf's summer program for English teachers provides occasion for an intense period of study, learning, and reflection. The National Council of Teachers of Mathematics' regional workshops build and sustain communities of math educators. University collaborations provide workshops that bring teachers together around a specific content area or skill set. District study groups flourish in many communities, joined by teachers from schools across the district interested in pursuing particular topics or literature. As valuable and important as these learning resources are for teachers' professional growth, school-based teacher learning communities make particular and indispensable contributions to teachers' learning and professional culture.

One reason why school-based teacher learning communities make a singular contribution is that sustained change in day-to-day practice is inherently local. Teachers need opportunities to identify and interpret weak classroom-based signals about problems of and for practice, and these signals only can be picked up at close range. Strong signals of the effectiveness of teaching and learning, such as aggregate evidence about patterns of student learning, of course provide important information. However, instructional improvement that benefits all students often rests on observations about such things as how various students respond to elements of a curriculum, or which students need reinforcement in particular skills—evidence available only through up-close attention to classrooms and students.

School-based teacher learning communities are positioned between "macro" or system-level directives and resources and the "micro" realities of teachers' classrooms. Thus, they are uniquely capable of interpreting, mediating, and conveying information from the larger system. They foster more coherent classroom practices because they represent community understandings, and more productive ones because they are situated in particular instructional settings. In other words, school-based communities of practice can manage from the middle to connect teachers' work to their larger system context in ways that are both more effective and efficient.

What Do School-Based Teacher Learning Communities Do?

School-based teacher learning communities are found at grade levels, within departments, or sometimes across a whole school. Ideally, they operate at multiple levels within a school, complementing and reinforcing teachers' work. Teacher learning communities within schools serve interrelated functions that contribute uniquely to teachers' knowledge base, professionalism, and ability to act on what they learn. Three such functions stand out: they build and manage knowledge; they create shared language and standards for practice and student outcomes; and they sustain aspects of their school's culture vital to continued, consistent norms and instructional practice.

Build and Manage Knowledge to Improve Practice

Teachers develop and acquire different kinds of knowledge in learning communities. Marilyn Cochran-Smith and Susan Lytle (1999) provide a valuable distinction in the types of knowledge that inform practice: *knowledge of practice*, or information about student performance, and *knowledge for practice*, or information about best practice.

As teachers inquire into students' work and explore connections between practice and outcomes, they create knowledge *of* practice. Learning communities provide opportunities for reflection and problem-solving that allow teachers to construct knowledge based on what they know about their students' learning and evidence of their progress. Generic problems of classroom practice become more concrete in the process—they take on names and faces. In this sense, learning communities build knowledge by providing a "social life" for information, a setting in which data can turn into new understanding through discussion and reflection (Brown & Duguid, 2000).

When teachers examine students' work together, it helps them consider how practice has been successful or fallen short of expectations. Though success can teach valuable lessons, teacher learning communities more often study failure or evidence of mismatch between standards established for students' learning and what students actually accomplish. Teachers use data about achievement gaps between expectations and outcomes—and unexplained differences in achievement among students of different racial, ethnic, or economic groups—to organize knowledge around concrete problems of practice. Evidence about the failures of classroom instruction motivates change. Strong teacher learning communities encourage teachers to report disappointing student outcomes, rather than hide them. Then they make the most of them through a critical review of practice.

As teachers rethink practice, knowledge *for* practice—formal knowledge and theory for teachers to use to improve their practice—is an essential asset. Such knowledge draws from the various outside resources available to the community (workshops, university partnerships, networks, and other expert-based opportunities) to learn about cutting-edge content and pedagogy, as well as state and professional association standards for student performance. A teacher learning community provides a forum in which teachers can translate knowledge from the environment—knowledge *for* practice—in terms specific to their students, subjects, and classroom settings. Helen Simons and colleagues (Simons, Kushner, & James, 2003) characterize this practice-based collective interpretation as "situated generalization." In this translation, teachers' knowledge *of* practice acts as a critical resource and complement to research-based knowledge. Communities of teacher learners build a storehouse of "best practices," and are able to assess the suitability of the alternative practices available to them. Donald Schön (1983) called this process the "reflective transfer" of knowledge. Teachers know not only what kinds of resources best suit their school, they also learn where they need to build or rebuild their own technical capacity. The community serves as both site and source of learning as teachers become active learners through processes of inquiry and deliberation. Communities of teacher learners adopt what Cochran-Smith and Lytle (1999) call an *inquiry stance* toward their own practice as well as their broader workplace environment.

Teacher learning communities also manage knowledge by sharing learning resources. Not all teachers participate in special project initiatives; only a portion of a school's faculty attends university workshops or participates in professional networks. A school-based learning community offers a forum in which everyone can use this "knowledge property." When these resources are brought into the school, it minimizes the instructional fragmentation that often results when some teachers have learning opportunities that others don't. Private knowledge becomes public knowledge. A school-based learning community also allows members to learn from one another's strengths, thereby boosting individual and collective know-how. Teacher learning communities build a faculty's *collective* capacity to provide high-quality, rigorous instruction to all students and so enhance capability to respond quickly and effectively to evidence of failure or surprises.

Teacher learning communities also may generate new knowledge about curriculum and pedagogy. They might, for example, explore the consequences of different instructional strategies, either with groups of students in a class or across classrooms. These efforts allow teachers to assess how alternative strategies work for their students, rather than consider them in theory or in settings different from their own. These teacher-led investigations also allow teachers to consider a broadened set of outcomes as markers of students' learning. Hence, they flag new possible problems. Ongoing learning and adjustment of practice found in school-based teacher learning communities make possible what Karl Weick and colleagues (Weick, Sutcliffe, & Obstfeld, 1999) call "collective mindfulness," or an ongoing watchfulness about how well students are doing. Collective mindfulness assumes continual evaluation, interpretation, and adjustment that are alert to unwanted or unexpected outcomes. Mindfulness checks inertia and complacency about practice and supports collective responsibility.

Create Shared Language, Vision, and Standards for Practice

In large schools especially, teachers use different terms to describe their practice. They seldom have a "community of explanation," where teachers share language and understanding about meanings of evidence and expectations (Freeman, 1999). A learning community develops shared language about their practice and commits to high-quality intellectual work for their students. In a vibrant learning community, teachers' practice and standards for students' learning are more in sync, in marked contrast to the variability one finds along the corridors of many American schools. Practice, traditionally teachers' private domain, moves into the public space of the learning community. As practice is "deprivatized," common understandings and expectations for practice promote coherent practices within and across grade levels. Teachers will be hampered in their efforts to integrate new ideas into their practice and deepen their work if their school (or relevant grade or department) operates on a contrary course or according to different professional norms.

Shared vision, collaboration, and learning together provide the foundation for teachers to take collective responsibility for students' success; the community's interdependent work structure allows teachers to act on this vision. An established teacher learning community makes the school accountable for student learning, rather than locating accountability exclusively in an external mechanism, such as the high-stakes testing systems used in many areas. The learning of all students becomes the responsibility of all faculty, rather than individual teachers only. Questions change as teachers assume norms of collective responsibility and a service ethic, moving from questions centered on an individual teacher's competence to assessments of community capacity: What is this faculty going to do about disappointing student outcomes? About significant achievement differences among groups of students? When this happens, ongoing learning and critical reflection become professional norms; practice synchronizes because teachers have clear, shared understandings of one another's classroom work. Understandings about collective responsibility promote collective growth. They also allow collective autonomy, or teachers' ability to act on their professional best judgment as they work with their students in their classrooms, because community norms and expectations are clearly understood.

Sustain School Culture

Community carries culture. A cohesive, vibrant teacher learning community protects against "flavor-of-the month" fads and shifting priorities by keeping the school, department, and grade focused on agreed-upon expectations and practices. In this way, it supports long-term instructional consistency. Learning communities also help socialize new teachers and administrators by reinforcing norms of practice among faculty and affirming expectations for teachers' ongoing learning and growth. A learning community provides the social interaction and informal learning opportunities necessary to incorporate new members and teach them about the standards, norms, and values that guide practice. Similarly, Adam Gamoran and colleagues (2003) conclude that inquiry within a community of teachers not only enhances teachers' knowledge and skills but also increases the social resources of the school.

EVIDENCE THAT TEACHER LEARNING COMMUNITIES BENEFIT STUDENTS

Teachers must learn new ways of teaching if contemporary schools are to meet society's demands that students acquire the competencies they need to participate in the knowledge society, and that all children learn to high standards. School-based teacher learning communities align with current empirical evidence of the most effective professional development strategies. As environments for learning, teacher communities exhibit all the features identified with effective professional development efforts (see Hawley & Valli, 1999). Researchers agree that teachers learn best when they are involved in activities that: (a) focus on instruction and student learning specific to the settings in which they teach; (b) are sustained and continuous, rather than episodic; (c) provide opportunities for teachers to collaborate with colleagues inside and outside the school; (d) reflect teachers' influence about what and how they learn; and (e) help teachers develop theoretical understanding of the skills and knowledge they need to learn.

Teacher learning of this stripe translates into enhanced student learning. A wide range of statistical data supports the claim that school-based professional learning communities improve teaching and learning. Evidence includes:

- Positive effects of teacher learning community measures on student achievement for both regional and nationally representative school samples
- Strong correlations of teacher learning community with teaching practices that predict students learning gains
- Strong correlations of teacher learning community and student experiences of their school and class.

Using data from the National Longitudinal Study of 1988 (NELS: 88),[1] Valerie Lee and colleagues conducted three studies that consistently showed that teacher community had a positive statistical effect on student achievement gains (Lee & Smith, 1995, 1996; Lee, Smith, & Croninger, 1997). Each study used sophisticated multilevel modeling techniques designed to estimate professional community and other school effects on student outcomes. All three studies support the hypothesis that students do better academically in a school where their teachers take collective responsibility for the success of all students. Further, these analyses showed that students' socioeconomic status had less effect on their achievement gains in schools with collaborative teacher communities; in other words, inequalities between students mattered less.

Another study using the NELS: 88 data base, conducted by Brian Rowan and colleagues (Rowan, Chiang, & Miller, 1997), analyzed effects of teachers' ability, motivation, and work situation on students' achievement. These analysts found that each factor had independent effects, with teacher control over instructional decisions and common planning time standing out as school predictors. Further, these school conditions correlate significantly with teacher expectations and other classroom instructional variables that predict student achievement.

Evidence from prior research indicated that analysis of teacher community effects on student learning would need to focus on the department level. Our analysis of teacher survey data on professional community showed more variation within high schools than between them (McLaughlin & Talbert, 2001). Using the Longitudinal Study of Youth (LSAY) national data base (a national research program that started with 7th graders in 1987), another group of researchers studied effects of teacher professional community on a range of student academic outcomes in math and science departments, with 53 high schools represented in the national sample (Yasumoto, Uekawa, & Bidwell, 2001). This study focused on the high school department level, analyzing data for math and science departments. They found that several conditions describing teachers' "professional discussion networks"—communication density, intensity of instructional practice norms, and consistency of practice—intensified the positive statistical effects of good teaching practices on student outcomes. The study provides statistical evidence to argue that teacher learning communities develop knowledge of practice that is beyond the sum of competent and innovative teachers.

Convincing evidence for the claim that teacher learning communities boost student learning also comes from the research of Fred Newmann and Associates (1996), in a study from the early 1990s using a national sample of restructured high schools. They developed elaborate survey and field measures of "authentic instruction," grounded in learning theory, in order to assess effects of instruction on student learning. They also captured teaching norms and teacher interaction through teacher survey measures of "professional community" (shared purpose, collaborative activity in teaching, collective focus on student learning, deprivatized practice, and reflective dialogue). Data for the 24 high schools show strong correlations between measures of authentic instruction and student achievement and between professional community and authentic instruction. These relationships show clear connections between how teachers work together and the learning opportunities they provide their students (see also Louis & Marks, 1998).

Our local analysis of teacher community effects on student achievement gains for a sample of schools participating in the Bay Area School Reform Collaborative (BASRC) showed statistically significant effects of a measure of school inquiry practices (Center for Research on the Context of Teaching, 2002). Students did better in schools where teachers examined student achievement data together and collaborated to develop and assess interventions.[2] Survey data for a small case study sample of nine schools showed strong correlations between (a) teacher ratings of collegial inquiry in the school and (b) student ratings of teacher–student respect, their active role in class, and their academic self-efficacy. Although this sample was small, these data capture the meaning for students of teachers' professionalism and their collaboration to improve teaching.

This book's analysis of professional community builds on this body of national and local research, showing statistical relationships and the effects of various measures of teacher learning community on teaching practice, how students experience learning opportunities, and student achievement gains.

Yet although an established, school-based learning community represents an ideal for practice, this vision is far from reality in most American schools. And teachers' school-based learning communities usually do not appear on menus of professional development or learning resources associated with the various efforts undertaken to reform the nation's schools. School-based learning communities are difficult to establish and sustain. Lack of trust, time, and talent are the usual reasons. When teachers are unwilling to take the risks that go along with candid reflection, when they don't have many opportunities to come together over students' work, when they lack leadership or expertise at the school site, then community-building initiatives are hamstrung and commitment erodes during faculty or leadership transitions. Certainly, efforts to mandate these professional relationships, and to mandate the norms of professionalism that underwrite them, have proven unsuccessful (Hargreaves, 1991). In large part, efforts to mandate community have failed because this kind of change cannot be commanded into existence. Teacher learning communities change culture in a way difficult to accomplish in any profession, but most especially in the isolated, individualistic lives of schoolteachers.

How might practitioners and policymakers cultivate and continue a vigorous learning community among a school's teachers? Although compelling evidence supports conclusions about the contribution and character of strong teacher learning communities, much less is known about how to start and sustain them. This book addresses these interrelated questions.

THE EMPIRICAL FOUNDATION AND
ORGANIZATION OF THE BOOK

We have studied teachers' workplace settings for many years. We have talked with teachers in staff rooms; observed them in classrooms; and attended workshops, staff meetings, and professional development sessions. We have interviewed and surveyed teachers and administrators in districts around the country. Some of this research has been problem-focused: How does context matter for teaching and learning? What is the district role in education reform? Other research has examined specific reform initiatives and sought to show how various efforts affected teachers and students. This body of research makes up the empirical foundation that informs this book.

The cases we feature are of several kinds: strong teacher learning communities in a high school department and an elementary school; effective facilitation of teacher community development in an elementary and a middle school; off-site professional development that supports teacher learning communities; and initiatives and designs that develop local capacity to support an agenda for teacher learning communities.

Our description of strong teacher learning communities features the mathematics department of San Lucio High School, which was one of our case study sites in a National Science Foundation–funded research project on high school department contexts of math and science education reform. When our 3-year project began in 1993, this department stood out for its highly developed teacher learning and improvement practices and for its effective, unconventional instructional program. The school's predominantly Latino and Asian-American students were taking more math classes and achieving at higher levels on performance assessments than was typical of schools with similar student demographics. This case illustrates how teachers in a department community can work and learn together to improve their students' math learning.

Paulsen Elementary School affords another look at a strong teacher learning community. This school, serving a predominantly Asian, Filipino, and Hispanic student population in a midsized district, has participated for 10 years in the Bay Area School Reform Collaborative (BASRC). The BASRC initiative was launched in 1996 with an Annenberg Challenge grant and matching funds from the Hewlett Foundation; it included 86 schools in its first 5 years. BASRC continued to work with 26 Bay Area districts after 2001 with grants from the Hewlett Foundation and several other local foundations. Its mission was to move school cultures toward a vision of professional learning communities—communities where data are used continually to improve the quality and equity of student learning. BASRC used the term "cycle of inquiry" to describe the process of using data to assess student outcomes, to evaluate and adjust instructional practices, and to measure the effects of new practices on student outcomes. We evaluated BASRC from 1996 through 2005;

during this period, we followed Paulsen Elementary School as a case study site. (See Center for Research on the Context of Teaching, 2002, for our evaluation of BASRC Phase 1.)

Two typical schools are the settings for our analysis of community-building strategies. One is a Bay Area middle school with a predominantly African-American, Asian, Filipino, and Hispanic student population; it joined BASRC in 2001. This case focuses on how an experienced BASRC facilitator developed the faculty's inquiry practices and enhanced its ability to change instruction; student outcomes improved significantly within a couple of years. The other, a high-poverty New York City middle school, is the setting for two case studies of community-building strategies. One case highlights community-building through subject content. It features the work of a consultant from the New York City Math Project (NYCMP) at Lehman College who facilitated the growth of teacher learning communities through on-site math team meetings, classroom consulting, and off-site classes. The other case highlights community-building through students and student work. It features the work of the co-director of the Elementary Teachers' Network (ETN). These teacher educators worked together in the middle school under the auspices of the Students at the Center (SATC) initiative.

The DeWitt Wallace-Reader's Digest Funds (now part of the Wallace Fund) launched SATC in 1996 as a 5-year professional development initiative. It aimed to increase the capacity of teachers in three large city school districts to teach in ways that would promote problem-solving, critical analysis, and high-order thinking among low-income students. Through an elaborate selection process, the foundation funded SATC projects in Chicago, New York, and Philadelphia. In each city, project designers selected several professional development organizations for their strong track record; they were funded collectively by the SATC project to work with 20 to 30 schools in the district. Our evaluation documented the range of professional development activities in each SATC project and followed the school-based work in four case study schools in each city over the course of the initiative (Burch, 2000; Center for Research on the Context of Teaching, 1999; Friedrich, 2001).

The SATC-Philadelphia summer practicum illustrates how off-site professional development supports teacher learning community. Philadelphia's SATC design included four organizations working with all schools in two of the district's clusters (a cluster includes all schools feeding into a particular high school; this governance structure has since been dismantled). Attempting to build upon Philadelphia's standards-based reform, under way in the district from 1996 to 2001, the partners worked collaboratively to develop cross-school resources for teacher learning communities. The summer practicum that involved teacher teams from each school was one such effort that helped build teacher learning communities.

Our discussion of a local learning agenda for teacher community development features the Parent Partnership, a Chicago-based SATC organization at work in one of our case study schools. Its success in building parent communities drew our attention to the kinds of strategies and practices it had developed to help parents make meaningful contributions to education reform. We also draw on SATC schools' work with parents in Philadelphia to illustrate how parents' learning contributes to and extends teachers' classroom efforts.

Finally, reform efforts in San Diego City Schools and a former New York City community school district support our analysis of district strategies to develop teacher learning communities. (New York City's 32 community school districts were consolidated into 10 super districts when Joel Klein assumed the Chancellorship in 2002.) This research was carried out as part of a 4-year project examining "reforming districts" (Hightower, Knapp, Marsh, & McLaughlin, 2002; McLaughlin & Talbert, 2002). Both districts invested in building professional learning communities at one or another level of the system; together, they help us learn about the challenges and potentials for change.

We build upon the above experience as well as other research to support our conclusion about the indispensable but generally ignored role of teachers' school-based learning communities. We illustrate the special value of teacher learning communities for practice and the profession. We also underscore various points in their development, warn of pitfalls on the road to change, and highlight promising approaches to developing teacher learning communities in the nation's schools.

Chapter 2 describes this form of professional community as a departure from typical school cultures, as an advanced stage of a community development process, and as it is embedded in school system contexts that more or less support and sustain it. Chapter 3 offers principles for how to develop learning communities. It illustrates how a facilitator can work with teacher groups to develop communities of practice, describes how principals support transitions between stages of school communities, and shows the tensions and challenges for changing school culture. Chapter 4 describes how high-quality off-site professional development supports the development and effectiveness of teacher communities in schools. We argue that building communities of practice in schools does not displace other forms of teacher professional development, as some might infer from evidence presented in other chapters.

Chapter 5 moves outside teachers' immediate professional communities to consider how others in the broader context affect teachers' learning and classroom consequences. The chapter shows how even the best-designed professional development resources will fall short, and the most robust professional community will falter and dissolve, when other elements in teachers' professional context ignore, frustrate, or work at cross-purposes with the learning and change they intend. Chapter 6 takes up the challenges and promising practices associated with carrying out a local learning agenda that includes key actors in broader contexts and informs them about teachers' work. Chapter 7 examines why, despite compelling evidence of their special value to teaching and learning, school-based teacher learning communities are not common in American schools—nor do policymakers feature them as ways to improve student outcomes. It considers how local school system contexts would need to change for such communities to develop and thrive.

2

Challenges of Re-culturing Schools into Learning Communities

Teacher learning communities are uncommon in U.S. schools. In fact, the norms and practices of this type of professional community depart significantly from teachers' work in typical elementary and secondary schools. This chapter addresses the challenges of re-culturing schools into learning communities. First we contrast teacher learning community with more common types of professional communities in schools, pointing to differences in their norms of instruction and collegial relations. We then describe teachers' work in two school learning communities—a high school department and an elementary school—illustrating how their professional practices depart from conventions in teaching. Next we describe developmental stages of school change toward teacher learning communities and problems of transition between them. Questions about developing school learning communities and contexts that shape potentials for school culture change frame subsequent chapters.

HOW TEACHER LEARNING COMMUNITIES DIFFER FROM TYPICAL SCHOOL COMMUNITIES

How teachers see their students, the subject matter they teach, their colleagues, their district, and their parent community are all colored by the culture of their up-close professional community. Teacher learning communities stand out for their strong commitment to serving all of their students well, innovation in subject instruction to improve student learning, and success in obtaining school and district resources and support for their collaborative work.

Teacher communities in U.S. schools can have qualitatively different teaching cultures—differing in their perceptions of students, student roles in the classroom, subject content, pedagogy, and useful assessments of student learning, as well in their norms for collegial relations and preferences for instructional policies. For example, in one high school we studied, teachers in the English department described their students as bright and engaged, while teachers in the social studies department saw their students as academically weak and unmotivated, underscoring the decline they had witnessed in recent years. In the English department, teachers work together daily to improve their courses and teaching. They use data on student learning to evaluate their instructional practices. They know and like their students as individuals and as learners. This faculty is proud of its track record, but always identifies targets for improvement, works with school administrators to get resources needed to support their learning and innovations, sees themselves as learners and as part of a department learning community, and participates in broader professional networks. They are committed to a career in teaching. In sharp contrast, teachers in the social studies department who teach in nearby classrooms work in isolation, and many have given up the struggle to improve courses and classroom instruction on their own. These teachers have been unsupported by their department chair and feel constrained by district policies, and many are considering a career change. Students in this high school feel the difference in these department professional cultures. In a survey, they gave significantly higher ratings to their English classes on teacher enthusiasm and support, challenging content, and the degree of effort that they (the students) put into learning in the class. In interviews and conversation, students talked about liking English and being supported by their teachers and about being bored and cutting classes in social studies. This contrast is striking because these department faculties teach the same students in the same organizational and civic community context.

At the elementary grade level, similar differences in teacher community culture surface between schools or between grade-level teams within the same school. For example, two K–5 schools, located eight blocks apart in a midsized urban district, developed widely divergent professional cultures. In one, teachers work together regularly on instruction in literacy and math in grade-level teams, with the principal and a literacy coordinator facilitating and providing resources for the faculty's learning and improvement efforts. In the neighboring school, teachers work in isolation and complain about their principal, their district, and the school's poor quality of teaching; they have little respect and trust for one another and are discouraged by their students' weak academic skills. In 2003–04, the latter school was classified for a third year as underperforming, while the nearby school with a strong learning community was meeting its improvement targets and surpassing the academic performance levels expected on the basis of student demographics.

Our analysis of teacher community patterns between and within the high schools and elementary schools we have studied over the past 15 years identified three general facets of professional culture that shape both students' and teachers' opportunities to learn. Teacher professional communities differ from one another in

- *Technical culture*: views of students, conceptions of subject content, beliefs about student learning, and understanding of effective pedagogy and assessment
- *Professional norms*: collegial relations, views of professional expertise, and conceptions of career
- *Organizational policies*: criteria for course or class assignments and resource allocation, for example.

Comparing teacher communities on these dimensions of teaching culture, we identified three types of professional communities—typical (weak) community, strong traditional community, and learning community (see Table 2.1). Contrasts among them highlight what is distinctive about teacher learning communities and reveal challenges for change.

Weak Professional Community

Teacher communities in American secondary and elementary schools generally are weak. A tradition of autonomy in teaching works against the formation of shared technical culture; teachers most often avoid discussing teaching and student learning and do not intrude into one another's classrooms (Little, 1982; Lortie, 1975; Smylie, 1994). Instruction in these communities is mostly conventional—text-focused and teacher-directed, with students working alone on routine assignments and graded on the curve. Absent conversations about instruction and leadership for improvement, teachers in such professional communities come to understand little about the principles and evidence that ground national and state standards for teaching and learning. They persist with practices that current research evidence deems ineffective. Many teachers water down the curriculum for students with weak academic skills in a well-intentioned attempt to make their classes fun or comfortable. In weak professional communities, teachers who work to engage all their

Table 2.1. How Teacher Communities Differ in Culture

Professional Community Type	Typical (Weak) Community	Strong Traditional Community	Learning Community
TECHNICAL CULTURE			
Belief about students	Students differ in ability to succeed academically	Students differ in ability to succeed academically	All students can achieve at high academic standards
Student role as learner	Passive role in content learning	Passive role in content learning; active role in advanced classes	Active role in content learning for all students
Content	Text-based subject content	Sequential, hierarchical subject topics and skills	Core discipline-based concepts spiraled through curricula
Pedagogy	Knowledge transmission; emphasis on text coverage	Knowledge transmission; emphasis on teacher lecture	Bridging subject and student knowledge; learning community
Assessment practices	Text-based homework and tests; curve grading	Special tests for screening and sorting students; curve grading	Performance assessments using standards-based rubrics; feedback for improvement
PROFESSIONAL NORMS			
Collegial relationships	Isolation enforced by norm of privacy	Coordination around student testing and assignment policies	Collaboration around teaching and learning; mentoring
Professional expertise	Expertise as developed through private practice	Expertise as based in discipline knowledge	Expertise as collective, based in knowledge shared and developed through collaboration
ORGANIZATIONAL POLICIES			
Teacher course/class assignment	Prerogative of seniority	Teacher tracking by expertise	Course rotation and sharing for equity and learning
Resource allocation	Tenure-based access to resources	Resource access according to teacher expertise and track	Collective definition of resource needs and sources; resource creation and sharing

Source: Adapted from Milbrey W. McLaughlin & Joan E. Talbert, *Professional Communities and the Work of High School Teaching,* Chicago: University of Chicago Press, 2001.

students in challenging subject content are the exception. The solo innovators sometimes find knowledge and support for innovation from professional networks outside the school, yet most become frustrated in their isolated efforts to improve student learning and discouraged from staying in the teaching profession.

A teacher in the weak social studies department mentioned earlier considered himself fortunate to have a job in a desirable suburban district and school, but felt isolated and became increasingly bored with teaching over the 3 years we followed him. He was considered by school administrators to be an innovative and highly effective teacher. He regularly brought newspaper articles to his classes and helped his students to make connections between current politics and American social history. He was a strong teacher in a weak department. He was disappointed that his colleagues didn't have the interest or time to discuss teaching or share lessons, and he became bitter over the fact that he alone was working to improve courses and students' engagement in history. After 8 years of teaching, he was tired from the hard work of keeping up in his field and adapting instruction to his students' needs by himself and talked about switching careers. He was unwilling to lower his expectations for his teaching and his students' learning.

Strong Traditional Community

Teachers in strong traditional communities coordinate their work around student assessments and decisions about student placements in classes and groups. This mode of practice breaks from traditional norms of privacy and appears to be triggered by a combination of accountability pressure and changing student population. The high school departments and elementary schools of this mode translate notions of standards-based instruction and accountability into coordinated programs for tracking courses or classes and assigning students and teachers to them. Teachers coordinate their work in terms of assessing student readiness to move on to more challenging instructional material. In elementary schools, this practice results in student grouping and reassignment based on the latest round of test scores. In high schools, it results in course tracking and high student failure and retention rates. Teachers in the strong traditional departments talk about the high failure rates in their classes as a sign of the department's uncompromising commitment to high standards.

Strong traditional communities also track teachers according to their expertise in their subject, assigning the least-prepared teachers to the lowest-performing students (Finley, 1984; Page, 1991; Talbert with Ennis, 1990). In these communities, teachers see their own learning in sequential terms, as a series of university courses and advanced degrees. Similarly, they have a hierarchical view of teacher knowledge and expertise for subject instruction that justifies tracking teachers by level of course content. The practice exacerbates inequalities in student performance, since low-performing students are matched with the teachers least prepared to accelerate their content learning.

Professional rewards and careers of teachers in these communities also are unequal. The most expert teachers receive high status and esteem from their colleagues, as well as opportunities to teach the most motivated and accomplished students in the school. In high schools and elementary schools with traditional professional cultures, the most accomplished teachers strongly endorse the assessments that screen student entry into their classes and are rewarded by their students' strong performance. In contrast, beginning or least-prepared teachers who are assigned to teach the lowest-performing students struggle to create effective interventions. These teachers come to see themselves as failures or the teaching profession as inhospitable to their professional success and their students' achievement.

In both weak teacher communities and strong traditional communities, beginning teachers lack collegial support while facing the most difficult teaching tasks. Many leave teaching within a few years. In the worst teaching situations in urban systems, some teachers leave before their first school year ends. Common conditions of professional practice in schools serving urban youth systematically undermine students' opportunities to learn to grade-level standards.

Glimpses of teaching and learning in weak and strong traditional teacher communities reveal both the importance and challenges of changing schools into learning communities. Developing teacher learning communities entails re-culturing schools—changing their technical culture, professional norms, and organization policies. This means that schools must confront prevalent beliefs that effective teaching is a matter of transmitting knowledge and that some students will not succeed, challenge privacy norms that inhibit teacher collaboration, and reorganize teachers' work so as not to reward experienced teachers with preferred teaching assignments. Schools in which teacher learning communities develop and thrive replace these constraints on teachers' and students' success with norms and practices that establish teachers' shared accountability for student achievement and collaboration to continually improve all students' success.

HOW DO TEACHER LEARNING COMMUNITIES IMPROVE STUDENT ACHIEVEMENT?

The work lives of teachers in school learning communities illustrate ways in which new professional cultures can be established to improve student achievement. Cases of a high school mathematics department and a K–8 school involved in the Bay Area School Reform Collaborative (BASRC)'s initiative to promote evidence-based reform show how particular professional practices replace the conventions in teaching that limit school success. The San Lucio math department and Paulsen Elementary School both developed into learning communities through a sustained reform process over several years. Here we highlight their practices as mature learning communities—how they build and manage knowledge to improve instruction, create shared commitments and standards for practice, and organize to sustain a culture of continual improvement. As elaborated in chapter 1, these key learning community functions establish the teachers' knowledge base, professionalism, and ability to act on learning that are essential to improved teaching and learning.

The San Lucio Math Department

San Lucio High School is one of two high schools in a district serving a working-class community in the San Francisco Bay Area; its students are predominantly Latino and Southeast Asian and come from the community's poorest neighborhoods. The math department began its reform in the late 1980s, in the wake of a state accreditation report that included evidence on multiple indicators of a failing math program. Student performance on state math assessments was generally poor, and large gaps existed between student racial and ethnic groups; students reported in surveys and focus groups that they couldn't learn in their math classes. San Lucio's math teachers were especially disturbed by the students' negative ratings of their teaching, and the math department launched an instructional improvement effort that continues today. The department's current practices of collaboration, norms of professionalism, and organization for equity represent a radical transformation from its culture in the late 1980s.

Collaboration on Mathematics Instruction

Presented with evidence that their traditional math classes failed students, the San Lucio math department embarked on a journey to improve teaching and learning. For more than a decade, the math faculty has assessed and refined its instructional program and practices in terms of student learning outcomes. They focus these assessments on students' conceptual understanding, problem-solving skills, mathematical reasoning, and ability to apply math concepts to real-world situations. Teachers redesign courses and lessons in light of evidence from their ongoing inquiry into student learning. In general, the faculty spirals key concepts through levels of math courses, enabling students to enter into learning the concepts at different levels of sophistication and to deepen their understandings of mathematical principles over time. Instruction is designed to promote student inquiry and probe their understandings of key concepts. Classroom assessments are ongoing, ensuring that both teachers and students get feedback in order to redirect their work. Further, the faculty has organized its program and instruction to advance all students through mathematics, including calculus (see Gutierrez, 1996, for further discussion of how math departments "organize for advancement").

These department practices challenge traditions of U.S. mathematics instruction that treat the curriculum as a sequence of topics, rely on texts and lectures for teaching, and assess students mainly for mastery of skills and procedures. They especially challenge practices of holding students back until they demonstrate readiness to move to the next level. The San Lucio math department not only rejected the practice of erecting hurdles for students' advancement, but also removed layers of remedial classes that their students would have to pass in order to enroll in Introduction to Algebra. In doing so they ignored the principle of "building blocks" as a metaphor for mathematics education, and as a result engaged increasing proportions of the school's students in higher-order learning.

Collaborative practices of the San Lucio math department include ongoing discussion among teachers about the successes and failures they experience in teaching particular lessons: What went well? Where were students struggling, and what didn't work as planned? These sorts of discussions are central to teachers' collaboration on improving math instruction.

To lay the groundwork for sharing such information and knowledge, the department organizes occasions for teachers to work in groups of two or three teachers to plan lessons focused on a particular math concept. For example, one group developed a lesson on quadratic equations, which they refined over several days of teaching and debriefing with each other. In sharing their learning during the regular department meeting that week, these teachers both contributed their polished lesson to their colleagues and stimulated discussion of how their experience transfers to teaching of related mathematical concepts.

San Lucio's math teachers improve student learning by working together on instruction at the intersection of particular students and particular subject content. The knowledge they develop includes how to represent concepts to students, how to detect learner misunderstandings and anticipate them, how to provide feedback that guides students' learning of particular concepts, and how to connect mathematics to students' experiences and aspirations. Ensuring that all students in the school are successful in mathematics defines the bottom line for teachers in this department.

In the early 1990s, the faculty began a comprehensive project to create heterogeneous math classes that would involve all their students in learning higher-order mathematical content. The department dismantled its math course tracking system and took up the challenge of teaching the same mathematics courses and content to students who varied widely in their math knowledge and skills. To this end, the faculty continually refines its curriculum and instructional practices. Teachers work to create multiple pathways into learning important mathematics concepts so that all students in their classes master higher-order learning. San Lucio teachers collaborate continually to invent new ways of accommodating their students' widely diverse math backgrounds in the classroom. They have earned a reputation in the region and state for their success in expanding students' access and achievement in mathematics.

Enforcing Norms of Professionalism

This department's strong service ethic distinguishes it from typical math departments. Teachers share a commitment to providing high-quality learning opportunities for all their students—a commitment to equity in math education that grounds their work with department colleagues and with students in the classroom. The department's reputation for closing gaps in students' math learning opportunities and achievement attracts teachers who share a strong commitment to equity; conversely, it repels teachers who view math learning as sequential and hierarchical and favor curricular tracking. San Lucio's math faculty believes that the department must reject traditional math education standards in order to uphold professional standards of service to their clients (the students) and accountability for quality.

Another norm of professionalism enforced by this math community is that which calls for continual learning. Teachers who join the San Lucio math department see themselves as lifelong learners in their field. This professional identity and readiness to join in the collective learning agenda of the department is important for sustaining the community, since teacher turnover in the school and district is quite high.

The department community's strong professionalism—its ethic of service to all students and commitment to continual learning and improvement—grounds its decisions about organizing teachers' work, as well as its instructional and learning practices, described above.

Organizing for Professional Learning and Equity

San Lucio's math department organizes its work to support and sustain teachers' learning and equitable student learning opportunities. Teachers collaborate on course teaching, new teachers are assigned mentors who model instruction and provide feedback in their classroom, and the faculty interacts regularly with math colleagues outside the school.

To develop shared expertise, the department created a policy of rotating course assignments among teachers and mentoring teachers new to a particular course. This practice improves the department's capacity to staff its advanced courses, while ensuring that teachers share responsibility for the least advanced courses. Rather than searching for teachers with experience in particular advanced courses, the department develops teachers' expertise in content instruction. These practices challenge prerogatives of seniority and credentials that create a pecking order for teacher assignment in traditional communities and weak communities alike. In the latter settings, teachers least prepared in the subject are marginalized, along with their students, in low-track classes.

This math department also developed an induction program that is locally regarded as exemplary. Unlike beginning teachers in typical high schools, who struggle on their own and are often assigned to "pay their dues" in the toughest assignments, San Lucio's new math teachers begin their careers with significant and sustained support. Beginning teachers are paired with experienced department colleagues and provided with a daily "prep period" to observe their senior colleague's instruction. The two plan and reflect on daily lessons in their respective classes. These teachers' opportunities to absorb the thinking and teaching practices of strong colleagues support their learning of instruction and the formation of their identity as mathematics educators.

Beginning teachers and newcomers to the school are folded into the department's culture and community practice. They participate in math faculty meetings devoted to reflection and problem-solving on classroom instruction. Through these conversations, newcomers learn the department's priorities and routines for collaborative work, shared repertoires of practice, and norms for sharing knowledge and requesting feedback. The department sustains its knowledge and learning practices by orienting new teachers to practices that the community has found to be successful with its students and bringing them into the ongoing work to improve math teaching and learning.

For the San Lucio math department, professional community boundaries are broad; they encompass math educators in universities and other high schools in the region and nation. Department faculty meetings regularly include outside math educators who join them to reflect on math instruction and design improvements. When the department detracked its math program, it formed an alliance with a university program with a strong research-based strategy for improving teaching and learning in heterogeneous classrooms. Teachers in the department are leaders in the California Math Council, and they participate in broader teacher education and K–12 math education networks in the region, state, and nation. These open department boundaries enrich teachers' professional careers and commitments and ensure a steady flow of knowledge resources into the community.

Paulsen Elementary School

Paulsen Elementary School is one of 12 elementary schools in a K–12 San Francisco Bay Area urban district. Its student population has become increasingly diverse in recent years, with the percentage of white native-English-language students declining from 58% in 1997–98 to 39% in 2002–03 and English language learners increasing from 11% to 24% during the same period.

During 6 years of involvement in BASRC, Paulsen developed a learning community that has fostered steady gains in its students' reading comprehension. The BASRC initiative funded schools to use a cycle of inquiry model of school reform, designed to develop learning communities that sustain continuous improvement in student learning and close achievement gaps. Although details of the model have changed slightly over time, the cycle of inquiry begins with student data to examine gaps in performance, then moves to questions of school and classroom practices that might account for the gaps, then moves to plans for change, then evaluates effects of the change on student outcomes, and finally refocuses improvement efforts. Teachers' analysis of student data figures prominently in this initiative, as in many efforts to build teacher learning communities.

In their first year as a BASRC school, Paulsen's faculty chose improving literacy as its "focused effort" and developed a 3-year goal that students would decode text with 95% accuracy and that 80% of the students would pass their comprehension assessment. The school looked carefully at data, sought new assessments when they found that their current ones did not measure what they wanted to know, and looked for achievement gaps between race, ethnic, gender, and grade-level groups in the school. A support provider trained teachers to determine whether or not these achievement gaps were statistically significant, thus helping them pinpoint real discrepancies in student performance.

Using Data to Focus Instructional Improvements

As a founding BASRC school, Paulsen began its inquiry-based school reform work in 1996. By looking closely at student achievement data and engaging in successive cycles of inquiry over several years, the faculty has continually refined its understandings of difficulties students are having in literacy and instructional approaches for addressing them. The more sophisticated their use of data, the more teachers have been able to develop questions and seek new challenges for improvement.

The school balances a whole-school focus on literacy with inquiry at grade and classroom levels. The principal explained that keeping inquiry cycles connected to the school's vision is a top priority.

> Whatever's happening in the classroom that a teacher is doing in terms of the cycle of inquiry has to be linked to overall school goals. . . . You need people to be involved in something in common . . . [or] there's nobody to help you debrief and talk deeply about what you might be doing. . . . While the whole-school vision remained, the teacher community moved the core of the inquiry work to the grade level. Teachers are personalizing and trying to affect their practice so that it impacts student learning and teacher practices.

Teacher inquiry and collaboration on improvement in this elementary school happen through multiple grade-level learning communities. For example, the six teachers in the second-and-third-grade teacher team at Paulsen developed a system for collaborating on instruction that involves assessing student learning and designing instruction and interventions for students who test below grade level. The teachers are divided into two pods, with three teachers sharing students for reading and math. Their instructional focus is on struggling second graders, grade-level second graders, and struggling third graders. Teachers collaborate on planning interventions for student groups and lessons. They review data from multiple kinds of assessments three times a year in order to group students into three different performance levels and to design instruction appropriate to their learning needs. They also evaluate the district-adopted curriculum programs for their adequacy to address student learning needs and plan lessons together to fill in gaps. For instance, given limited attention to writing in their district-adopted Houghton Mifflin program, the team designed a writing task for their students that became the basis for student-led conferences with parents. Teachers collaborated on planning and assessing this assignment and using it to refine their practice as a grade-level team (see Young, 2004, for further analysis of teacher community practices in Paulsen Elementary School).

Paulsen's inquiry strategy has changed classroom practice across the school, and reading comprehension scores have risen. All teachers in this professional learning community can point to particular ways in which student performance has advanced through their collaboration to improve literacy instruction. One teacher described her second graders' improved writing performance:

> The whole class had interviewed me about Hawaii. They had taken notes and written paragraphs on it. And they were so well structured, so well organized—excellent writing. The quality of this writing was just amazing even compared to some of the things our fourth graders do. I think already people are starting to see little things all over the place.

Enforcing Norms of Professionalism

Like the San Lucio math department and other teacher learning communities we studied, the Paulsen elementary school faculty consistently expressed a strong collective commitment to serving all their students well. A service ethic was at the center of their community culture. Said one teacher, "Everybody's now at the point where it's like, 'Okay, these are our students.' It's not 'my class' and 'her class.' It's 'They're *our* students.'" Over several years, teachers in the school have developed commitment and trust in their shared accountability for all students' success in achieving high standards of academic performance. This service ethic and mutual accountability contrasts with conditions in weak and traditional school communities where teachers often vie for classes with high-achieving students.

At the root of this professionalism in Paulsen is the teachers' practice of using evidence to weigh their instruction against student achievement and working together to make improvements. The cycle of inquiry sustains the teachers' strong service ethic because it provides them with evidence that all students' learning can be improved through this process of inquiry and change.

Organizing for Professional Learning and Equity

Paulsen Elementary organizes its work to support shared leadership for data-based inquiry. Teachers developed a communication process that includes dialogue and measures consensus on decision issues. The school redesigned staff meetings so that teachers, rather than the principal, facilitate discussions on decision-making, professional development, and the cycle of inquiry. Further, the school designated staff development days for teacher teams to work on inquiry. The second-and-third-grade team had five full-day instructional meetings funded by BASRC and also met during common prep times and over lunch.

Instructional coherence became an explicit goal for the Paulsen school community. Teachers began to see what issues and projects fit with, or distracted from, their reform focus. A reform leader in Paulsen Elementary explained, "You can make an argument for anything to be connected to increasing student achievement, but we just want [to be] more direct. Either we need to make it more connected or cut it out." The school created an "alignment team" of teachers and administrators that used the cycle of inquiry to examine how effectively the school served its students on a range of indicators of academic and personal outcomes. This school team's inquiry spanned grade levels and went beyond academic performance data to identify areas for schoolwide improvement.

These organizational policies and structures enable teacher collaboration on instructional improvement. They direct the school staff to study data on teaching and student learning, and then to agree about next steps for changing instruction and for examining effects of change on student learning. They broaden school leadership for inquiry-based reform and limit teachers' dependence on outside support providers. A focus on coherence in reform practices aligns efforts across grade-level teams within the school and sustains the faculty's inquiry practices over time.

Paulsen teachers' capacity to use data effectively to evaluate and improve their teaching and school policies developed over a period of 5 years, with support from a highly skilled reform coordinator funded by BASRC. The school's steady movement toward learning community practices was unusual; in most cases, schools did not make a full transition from conventional culture to the norms and practices of teacher collaboration, learning, and change.

STAGES OF LEARNING COMMUNITY DEVELOPMENT AND CHALLENGES OF TRANSITION

Schools that become teacher learning communities move through stages and successfully address challenges for transition between them. Cross-case analysis of 10 BASRC schools provides evidence of a developmental trajectory of learning communities—qualitative shifts entailed in moving from conventional school culture to mature learning community practice. This analysis also points to particular problems of transition between community stages.

The BASRC initiative prescribed processes for developing learning community practices and funded schools for a period of 3 to 5 years to use data schoolwide to improve student achievement and close gaps. Although selected through an application process that focused on commitment to undertake inquiry-based reform, BASRC-funded schools began with varied reform histories and readiness to benefit from the cycle of inquiry model. Differences in the schools' cultures and practices after 5 years in the initiative reveal three broad stages of teacher learning community development, which we label *novice, intermediate*, and *advanced* stages. They represent qualitatively different ways of using data to improve school community practice, with different degrees of effectiveness.

Novice Stage

As they began the inquiry process, teachers in all 10 schools that we followed struggled to determine what pieces of baseline data would best help them understand students' progress and problems. All schools were at the novice stage at the beginning of the initiative; some schools never moved beyond it. In this stage, teachers confronted the demands imposed by new expectations and requirements. They wrestled with questions about what would "count" as evidence and what signaled progress. Schools that lacked a relevant reform history especially struggled to move beyond the initial stages of being overwhelmed and frustrated with all of the new tasks and demands associated with inquiry. Collecting baseline data throughout the school was the first step in their inquiry process.

In their first years of reform work, schools often spent most of their time and resources on data collection. Once the data were collected, the sheer amount of it often overwhelmed the schools. One reform leader explained, "I have suitcases of data—literally. That's how I move it from meeting to meeting." The schools often did not know how to move from data collection to using the data as evidence to examine questions about practice. Teachers in some schools became paralyzed by fears about what the data might reveal. The data could reveal that a school was sliding backward rather than moving forward. Or it could show that a particular teacher's class was not progressing as well as others. During a conference session, BASRC schools shared their fears with one another—fears of being judged, concern that data might make more work, fears of retribution if the school failed to reach its goals, and anxieties about lowering the teaching community's self-esteem if measurable growth was not achieved.

Moving through a cycle of inquiry require teacher communities to develop a repertoire of research skills, including constructing research questions, problem statements, and strategies for analysis. A few schools got stuck, never progressing beyond the novice stage. But for those that did progress, developing new expertise, norms, and expectations about data was a reinforcing process where success with inquiry fostered appetite for more data and analysis. Once schools were able to use data in a meaningful way, the evidence-based change process began to accelerate.

Novice schools worked to create systems to manage data and began to understand the value of inquiry for improving practice. At schools that did not yet possess broad-based leadership, a strong reform coordinator who fostered knowledge-building among teachers and an administrator who supported the development of trust and collaborative norms were key to moving a school from the novice to the intermediate stage. Challenges for leadership in the transition from the novice to the intermediate stage of community development included developing teachers' technical skills and comfort in using data for inquiry, establishing an atmosphere of mutual trust and respect, and supporting collaboration around inquiry.

Intermediate Stage

Schools that moved from the novice to the intermediate stage in their inquiry practices had begun to use the cycle of inquiry process to build a teacher community that included broad-based leadership. Schools gained comfort and competence when small improvements in student outcomes provided visible connections between inquiry and improved teaching and learning. These indications of reform progress increased teachers' consensus about the nature of the problem at their site and the limited range of responses to the problem. Yet intermediate-stage schools did not connect inquiry with practice easily. Instead, they struggled to shift the culture in their school toward reflection, evidence-based decision-making, and collaboration.

Schools in the intermediate phase of developing inquiry practices worked on clarifying shared goals for their students and building a common vision for the school. Part of this process included the development of shared language, or a "community of explanation" (Freeman, 1999), through which teachers could come to common understandings about teaching and learning. BASRC's cycle of inquiry required teachers to develop a shared vocabulary and understanding about their reform work as grounds for deepening their inquiry practices and making connections to their classroom practice. Inquiry was becoming ingrained in the processes of school decision-making and discussions of practice.

BASRC schools attempting to build a schoolwide learning community found that teachers learned inquiry processes at different rates. For instance, new teachers struggled to learn inquiry practices while mastering all other aspects of becoming a good teacher. Some teachers resisted school leaders' efforts to involve them in this reform work. In the words of one teacher, "I feel like saying, 'Leave me alone. I don't want to deal with the reflection. I have work to do.'" These teachers regarded the cycle of inquiry as an "add-on" to their already busy schedules; some viewed it cynically as the latest entry in a reform parade. Absent evidence of improved student outcomes through inquiry, these teachers focused on the time demands it imposed. Schools at this stage had not developed an overarching professional culture of inquiry. While some teachers formed learning communities, others opted out or remained at the novice stage.

During the intermediate stage of inquiry, faculty became less reliant on external agents for knowledge and ideas. They gained confidence in their ability to learn from their own school's inquiry work. At the same time, they were becoming more discriminating consumers of outside knowledge. If a support provider's services did not align with their newly honed focus, they severed ties with that organization. These schools developed their own knowledge as they became more aware of their own abilities and more targeted on the types of learning they needed to move forward in their focused efforts.

Teachers in schools at the intermediate stage of inquiry began to see that the data they collected were just the first step in the process. A high school teacher commented, "Data in and of itself isn't useful. It's what you do with it. Before we had data, probably we could have guessed that a lot of those things were the case. But once you formalize it, that implies that you have to do something." Once fears about how data could be used dissipated, data became a resource for identifying and addressing problems. Discourse about student achievement and evidence-based problem-solving became more frequent in the intermediate schools.

Connecting student outcomes to classroom practices challenged all BASRC schools. As intermediate-level schools developed the capacity to work with data, they often found data useful for locating problems, but not for identifying solutions. One high school teacher explained, "Forty percent of the students are not passing [at our school]. It's sort of like a statement. We don't know exactly what to do with it because people have not been trained on how to take [this understanding] back to the classroom." Without a sense of how to tackle particular problems revealed by the data, many teachers became frustrated with the inquiry process as a means to improve practice. In general, inquiry did not influence instruction in an ongoing, iterative manner in schools at this stage.

Many BASRC schools were stuck at this stage of community development after several years. They used the cycle of inquiry as one tool in a toolbox of school reform practices and did not deepen cycles of questioning, reflection, and action. Teachers in these schools learned procedural knowledge of inquiry practices, but not the principles and professional stance of inquiry (regarding this distinction, see Argyris, 1982).

Further, schools at this stage had not developed a strong norm of collective responsibility and service ethic to drive and sustain their progress on inquiry-based reform. Without this normative context, new practices for data use did not develop teacher learning communities. The schools thus faced technical, cognitive, and normative challenges for moving beyond the intermediate stage of inquiry: learning how to manipulate and read data, understanding principles of data-based inquiry and reform, and instilling a norm of collective responsibility for improving teaching and learning in the school.

Advanced Stage

Schools considered to be at an advanced stage had come to function as cultures of inquiry, or professional learning communities. Teachers had incorporated into their work the *process* of developing questions, collecting and analyzing data, and taking action based on that analysis. They judged the success of their inquiry by the extent to which it produced "actionable knowledge" that was useful in their classrooms (see Brown & Duguid, 2000, for a discussion of this kind of knowledge). The whole school had become both the site and focus for change, with inquiry extending into subject departments or grade-level teams and into classrooms. Teachers in these schools said they "couldn't imagine going back" to a professional stance or discussion about practice that was not evidence-based.

In the advanced-inquiry schools we studied, faculty discussions often probed deeply into patterns of student outcomes. They posed questions such as: Why do Black and Hispanic students differ in what they accomplish in upper elementary grades? Why do 10th-grade Latino boys consistently fall off in mathematics? Why are students' writing skills in one third-grade class more advanced than in the others? Teachers in these schools posed such questions without finger-pointing or blame, but in an effort to understand connections between classroom practices and what their students were able to do.

The use of inquiry to inform changes in classroom instruction distinguished schools at this stage of community development. Teachers conducted inquiry at classroom and departmental levels to find how particular curricula and instructional practices were linked to student outcomes and particular achievement gaps. They also sought and used knowledge of best practices as a part of their ongoing collaboration to improve instruction in the school. They used BASRC and other professional networks to point them to interventions designed to address the particular problems they identified through inquiry, and they looked for evidence that an intervention is effective with students like their own.

Shared language reflected the strength of the schools' technical culture around inquiry. While intermediate-stage schools had begun the process, advanced-stage schools had built a vocabulary around inquiry that figured prominently in teachers' conversations. As one high school teacher explained, "We have a common language at this school. At [my previous] school, there was only a very small group of people who understood what an outcome was, what a standard was, what a rubric was. I could only have a conversation with three people about those things. Here, there's a possibility for these conversations anywhere in the school." This shared language and understandings created the basis for schoolwide conversations about how data and research would inform decisions and plans for the future.

As the teacher community developed capacity to generate reform ideas and practices, teachers more carefully considered the knowledge resources they needed from outside the school. They became more selective in soliciting professional development and other outside coaching resources. They tended to seek external resources for specific instructional improvement targets—such as writing instruction in the primary grades or adolescent reading instruction across the curriculum—that fit within the school's broader work plan and inquiry cycle. In this sense, they ensured coherence of their improvement efforts and got strategic support where needed.

In addition to becoming better consumers of knowledge and support providers, advanced schools used inquiry tools to manage external pressures. For example, when concerned about state assessments, one school used a staff development session to assess the congruence between state standards and the school's reform focus. Each grade level listed the curricula they currently taught that met their own school's reform work and the curricula that met the state standards. Then they discussed the gaps and overlap in the current instructional practices across grade levels and how to address issues that surfaced.

At this stage of learning community development, teachers' conversation and use of evidence on student performance had moved to analysis of student learning patterns and to higher-order questions about *why* particular instructional practices are or are not working. Discussions about teaching and learning were grounded in evidence and analysis, rather than opinion or preconceptions. These professional norms and practices opened up the possibility of changing the conventions of teaching that generally are take for granted. They also turned around notions of accountability, shifting responsibility from the individual teacher to the teaching community.

A sense of collective responsibility for students' success was widely shared among teachers in the advanced schools. From this stance and service ethic, they were able to tackle tough questions of professional norms, beliefs about race and equity, and expectations for student and teacher learning. Teachers generally discussed disappointing student outcomes in terms of the school's community of practice, not in terms of individual teacher practices. They were able to speak objectively about issues that before had been seen as personal and subjective evaluation and to wade into difficult waters of equity and links with practice. Teachers' mutual accountability was a clear marker for schools advanced on inquiry, and a foundation for their continual learning and improvement.

Table 2.2 summarizes the three stages of community we found in our analysis of school progress on inquiry-based reform. Schools' capacity to

Table 2.2. Developmental Levels of Inquiry-Based Reform

	Novice	Intermediate	Advanced
Teacher Community	Constructing a teacher community; developing collaboration norms	Developing a norm of questioning; beginning to develop a shared language/ community of explanation	Becoming a learning community focused on improved practice and shared accountability
Shared Leadership	Developing systems to manage reform work	Broadening teachers' leadership roles in reform	Establishing ownership of reform work among most of faculty
Focused Effort	Creating a focused effort to guide school reform efforts	Clarifying vision; developing work plans to enact vision	Establishing coherence of school reform efforts; managing external pressures
Data Use	Discovering value of data and how to use it	Managing data so that it can be used in better ways	Developing systems for managing data
Inquiry Procedures	Experimenting with inquiry and creating procedures	Focusing on teaching and learning; identifying indicators of student progress	Connecting whole-school, subunit, and classroom inquiry focus and practices

confront challenges entailed in developing professional learning communities depends upon the knowledge and skills of teacher community facilitators and broad school leadership for change (Gamoran et al., 2003; McLaughlin & Talbert, 2001). Further, the likelihood that these favorable school conditions develop depends upon district, state, and federal policy environments and the messages and resources they convey to teacher communities, as well as upon cultures and capacities in broader local contexts of teaching.

Do schools and districts invest in skilled teacher community facilitators to nurture culture change? To what extent are a service ethic and learning agenda of teacher professionalism promoted within and beyond school systems? Are evidence-based standards for content instruction established to guide teacher communities' development and learning? Is there public commitment and civic capacity to nurture and sustain local investment in teacher professional development to ensure all students' learning? The chapters that follow take up these questions.

3

Developing Communities of Practice in Schools

Given evidence that teacher collaboration on instruction improves the quality and equity of student learning, why have education policy systems invested so little attention and resources in developing school-based teacher learning communities? Although some popular policies are consistent with this goal, they fail to engage the problem of changing school culture. For example, many districts have decentralized professional development resources in response to calls for "job-embedded" teacher learning opportunities; yet most provide little direction or support to school leaders for developing a culture of learning and improvement. Likewise, districts that have restructured their high schools into Small Learning Communities (SLCs) rarely provide guidance or resources to support teacher collaboration on instruction within the new units. Such district policy trends respond to evidence that teacher collaboration promotes student achievement, but they ignore the challenges entailed in developing professional learning communities.

The literature on teacher learning community also is mostly silent on the matter of how schools develop these productive professional norms and practices. Despite rich descriptions of the ways in which a school learning community works to improve instruction and student achievement, evidence is scant concerning the conditions and processes of its development. What strategies and resources are effective for building and sustaining collaborative professional communities in schools?

Research on the contexts of professional learning communities identifies a range of conditions that support and sustain them, such as state and district standards for teaching and learning in subject areas, on-site professional development time, and external professional networks. Yet these conditions are insufficient for the *development* of learning communities because they do not bring about change in the culture of teaching.

In schools that have all of the desirable context conditions, most teachers still practice in isolation from one another. Similarly, changing the structure of schools to promote teacher collaboration does not create learning communities. In a national study of restructured schools, Fred Newmann and associates (1996) concluded that a school's culture determined the effects of structural change on instructional practices, rather than the reverse. In other words, while existing teacher learning communities made good use of structural changes that supported their collaborative work, the restructuring of schools did not change professional cultures.

How do teacher learning communities develop in schools, then? Our research on reform initiatives with a mission to create school learning communities and on literature on community-building in business organizations suggest three broad conclusions about the processes of changing school culture:

- A teacher community of practice develops through *joint work on instruction*, usually starting with a focus on one facet of instruction—subject content, students, or assessment of student learning
- Teacher learning in a community depends upon *how well the joint work is designed and guided,* or the extent to which an effective learning environment is created for the teachers
- Teacher learning community development, spread, and sustenance depends upon proactive administrator support and broad teacher leadership.

This chapter elaborates and offers evidence in support of these broad conclusions. First we describe principles for practice to develop teacher learning communities, and to support learning in communities, that derive from research within and beyond education. Then we describe three cases of teacher learning community development in typical schools that illustrate the principles in action. Finally, we examine the roles that administrators play in supporting and sustaining the growth of teacher learning communities and the challenges entailed in changing school culture.

GETTING STARTED: PRINCIPLES FOR DEVELOPING COMMUNITIES OF PRACTICE

Developing teacher learning communities entails, first, the creation of joint work, or a project that engenders collaboration among a group of teachers who share a mission to improve instruction for their students (see Wenger, 1998, for analysis of communities of practice in various occupations and kinds of organizations). Such work could be, for example, designing an instructional unit on fractions, or developing a rubric for assessing student compositions, or developing an intervention for students with weak reading comprehension skills. Further, developing teacher learning communities entails the growth of learning practices, or the capacity of the group to create and use knowledge and tools for improving instruction with its students.

In all instances of significant school culture change that we found, leadership from within or outside the school was involved in getting the community development process started. This observation dovetails with the finding from research on community-building in business that a skilled "community coordinator" is key to developing an effective community of practice (Wenger, McDermott, & Snyder, 2003, p. 80). The coordinator convenes a group of individuals around a mission to improve organizational productivity and then focuses the group's collaborative efforts. A coordinator works to

- Identify important issues to focus the community's work
- Plan and facilitate community events
- Informally link community members with one another, promoting communication across organizational units and brokering knowledge exchanges
- Manage the boundary between the community and the formal organization, ensuring their authority and access to needed resources
- Foster the development of community members as individual learners
- Help build the practice of group learning—including the knowledge base, lessons learned, best practices, tools and methods, and learning events
- Assess the health of the community and evaluate its contribution to members and the organization.

The first four roles involve *organizing the community's work* (that is, determining the focus and boundaries for joint work), while the last three pertain to *establishing an effective learning environment* for the community. These general coordinating roles and functions also are entailed in developing teacher learning communities in schools.

Organizing Teachers' Collaborative Work

Getting teachers started on a course of collaborating to improve student learning takes a committed and skilled leader or facilitator. It often involves a precipitating event or evidence that existing instructional routines are not working for students in the school. Because traditions and conditions of teaching push toward autonomy, teachers need a compelling reason to begin collaborating to improve instruction. In the San Lucio math department featured in chapter 2, for example, teachers taught in isolation until they were presented with evidence that their students were dissatisfied and struggling in their math classes. Student complaints about math that surfaced in a school accreditation review in the early 1990s prompted teachers to reconsider their instruction and define a collective agenda to improve instruction.

The math department chair led the change process, facilitating the math faculty's development of goals and collaborative projects to address student needs and improve math instruction in the school. During the beginning phase of their collaborative work, the teachers agreed upon new norms and practices for the department. The chair reserved faculty meeting times for instructional rather than administrative work. As the community leader, she focused the group's discussion on problems for instructional improvement. When teachers disagreed, she facilitated their dialogue and defined dissension and occasional conflicts as normal and healthy aspects of invention and change. In her position of authority, she enforced group decisions about improvement efforts and garnered resources, such as release time and stipends, to enable teachers to observe each other's classes and to participate in off-site professional development in support of the department's learning. After such community practice had become routine, and when the chair retired several years later, the math faculty reflected on the kinds of leadership roles they would need to replicate in order to sustain their learning community and then decided how to distribute the roles among themselves. For example, they decided that a department leader would need to keep them on task in assessing student learning outcomes and designing and evaluating interventions. Teachers felt confident that their shared norms would sustain their work to improve instruction without the strong facilitation that their department chair had provided in the past.

Leaders of teacher community development in schools we studied held a wide range of positions within and outside the school system. They included high school department chairs, teacher leaders released half-time and full-time, district coordinators and content coaches assigned full-time or part-time to a school, teacher educators from a professional development organization or university, and support providers from an intermediary reform organization. Job titles attached to the role varied as well. Across the initiatives we studied, "professional developer," "consultant," and "partner" were titles used by the professional development organizations involved in Students at the Center (SATC), such as the Philadelphia Writing Project and the New York City Math Project; BASRC used the term "reform coordinator" and later "coach" to refer the individuals funded to facilitate inquiry-based school reform. In describing cases from these initiatives, we use their own terms. Otherwise we use the term "community facilitator" to refer to an individual who coordinates teachers' joint work and guides their learning.

Community-building is not just about creating or defining new work for teachers to do collaboratively. It is also about changing a school's professional culture. The effectiveness of a community facilitator depends upon the individual's skills in this role and upon the authority they have or are granted to lead school change. Once legitimized as a leader of change in the school, skilled facilitators can establish new norms of teaching—reflection on teaching with colleagues and co-designing interventions to better meet student needs. Community facilitators create a focus, rationale, and vehicle for teachers to depart from private classroom practice.

Promoting Learning in the Community

Skilled teacher community facilitators guide the group's learning and improvement practices. They establish conditions of effective learning environments for teachers (Bransford, Brown, & Cocking, 1999), ensuring that they are

- *Knowledge-centered,* focusing learners on problems and practices designed to deepen their conceptual knowledge and skills in a content domain
- *Learner-centered,* attending to individual learners' interests, cultural backgrounds, prior knowledge, and skills in order to create effective bridges for learning new content
- *Assessment-centered,* creating opportunities for learners to get ongoing feedback on their performance to guide their learning
- *Community-centered*, involving peers in joint work that draws

upon each person's knowledge and skills to build new understandings and practices.

For teachers as learners, the focus and content for learning center on how to create effective learning environments for students—classroom instruction that is centered on discipline knowledge and skills, on individual learners, on assessment, and on peer learning community. Community facilitators thus face the dual challenges of focusing and supporting teacher learning toward these goals for classroom instruction and also of creating these conditions for teacher learning.

As the cases in this chapter illustrate, skilled facilitators create occasions for teachers to work together on one or another facet of classroom instruction—subject discipline, students, or assessments. Any one of these starting places can focus the initial development and learning of teacher communities. A facilitator using subject content as the entry point might work with a group of teachers on teaching and learning fractions or, more broadly, on constructing bridges between the district's elementary and middle-grade mathematics programs. A facilitator using student work as a starting place might work with teachers to analyze a particular student's writing over time or focus on a student who is struggling in a math class. A facilitator using assessment data as the entry point for community-building might work with teachers to analyze the content dimensions underlying a literacy achievement gap between race and language groups. These foci for teacher community work represent potential multiple entry points for changing a school community.

Community facilitators bring particular knowledge, skills, and tools for engendering and supporting teachers' joint work. BASRC reform coordinators, for example, used the initiative's cycle of inquiry tool to help teachers focus on student assessment data (for details see Center for Research on the Context of Teaching, 2002; McLaughlin & Mitra, 2003). Consultants in SATC used particular designs for looking at student work, such as the descriptive review of a child (for information about a range of protocols, see McDonald, Mohr, Dichter, & McDonald, 2003). Facilitators who led with subject disciplines brought particular designs and tools for their work with teachers that were developed in organizations such as national and local writing projects and math projects.

Well-designed group activities and protocols are insufficient, however, to spur change in teaching cultures toward community practice. For example, many BASRC schools used the initiative's protocol for data-based inquiry in superficial ways that preserved teachers' private practice.

Similarly, in a district initiative that required grade-level teacher teams to use a particular lesson study protocol, most teams made only ritual use of the protocol, and few developed as learning communities through the lesson study process. Absent skilled guidance in using a particular protocol, a group's learning is likely to be procedural and shallow—what Chris Argyris (1982) termed "single loop learning"—and cannot move teachers toward collaborative efforts to improve instruction.

Three cases of skilled facilitation of teacher learning in schools describe guiding principles and practices for developing professional learning communities. The cases point to alternative "curricula" as entry points for teacher community-building—assessment data, individual students, and subject discipline. Further, they raise questions about strategies of beginning with a small voluntary group of teachers versus beginning with a whole school faculty.

DEVELOPING COMMUNITIES OF TEACHING PRACTICE: CASE ILLUSTRATIONS

A Bay Area middle school involved in BASRC and a New York City middle school involved in SATC show how school teaching cultures can change. The community facilitators who worked to build teacher learning communities in these schools include: (a) a Bay Area district teacher leader who worked as reform coordinator with a whole middle school faculty on evidence-based practice, (b) a co-director of the Elementary Teachers' Network (ETN), who worked with an interdisciplinary teacher study group as a consultant to the New York City middle school, and (c) a consultant from the New York City Math Project (NYCMP) who worked with this school's math teachers. In each case, the facilitator aimed both to deepen teachers' knowledge and skills in a particular domain of instruction—assessment, students, and subject discipline, respectively—and to develop norms and practices of teacher collaboration to improve teaching and learning.

Table 3.1 summarizes designs for community-building represented by these cases. The boundaries for teacher community and the nature of the facilitator experience and skills differed across the cases, as did the curriculum and materials that focused the teachers' work. The schools' different entry strategies for building teacher learning communities—particularly whether teacher participation was voluntary or involved the whole faculty—posed different challenges for change and presented dif-

Table 3.1. Designs for Developing Teacher Learning Community
            in Schools: Case Illustrations

Focus of Teacher Community Work	Assessment (Data-based inquiry)	Students (Learner-focused inquiry)	Subject Content (Math teaching and learning)
Community Boundary	Whole school	Interdisciplinary study group	Math teachers
Agent(s) for Community Development	School reform coordinator Literacy professional developer	Professional developer as consultant	Math educator as consultant
Tools and Knowledge Resources	Cycle of inquiry tool State/district/school assessment data Literacy professional development, off-site Literacy support provider BASRC coach network	Process for looking at student work Shared readings Classroom artifacts, observations, narratives about practice Elementary Teacher Network; SATC partners	CMP curriculum Math education class (taught by consultant) New York City Math Project; SATC partners Math professional networks and standards

ferent demands for school leadership

The cases reveal each entry strategy's particular benefits and challenges for changing a school's professional culture. They especially show how facilitators nurture the development of teacher learning communities and support their learning and instructional improvement.

Assessment Data as Entry

As schools are increasingly held accountable for improving student achievement and closing achievement gaps, teachers are pressed to use data on student learning to evaluate and improve their instruction. Yet teachers generally have little preparation or experience in analyzing student assessment data for the purposes of making instructional decisions. Many districts have responded by developing data systems that enable teachers to analyze trends in their students' performances on a range of assessments, and some provide technical training on data use for coaches, teacher leaders, or administrators. Professional norms that oppose accountability linked to standardized test data, however, can thwart teachers' use of data (for example, see Ingram, Louis, & Schroeder, 2004). Even under the ideal conditions where teachers have good access to student assessment data and are committed to using them, they still must develop skills in analyzing and interpreting the data in order to design programmatic and instructional responses. Teachers rarely have access to professional development adequate for developing these technical, interpretive, and design skills.

Since 1996, BASRC has tried to foster schoolwide learning communities and improve teaching and learning through teachers' use of student assessment data and systematic inquiry into sources of achievement gaps. The initiative's theory of action assumes that faculty discussion of disaggregated student achievement data will foster collective responsibility for closing gaps between student groups and will be a vehicle for evaluating and improving instruction and school policies. BASRC schools' varied success in implementing this reform strategy reveals what it takes to build school learning communities through evidence-based practices. Schools that made significant progress did so with expert guidance from one or more reform coordinators. In turn, as noted earlier, they achieved significantly greater student learning gains than schools where this strategy was not well implemented (Center for Research on the Context of Teaching, 2002).

The BASRC reform coordinator works with teachers to develop a culture and practice of using evidence to make decisions about instruction and school policy. The person in this role guides the faculty in using data on student outcomes to assess gaps in performance between student groups that differ in race, national origin, and English language status and to link those gaps to instructional practices. BASRC assumes that the school inquiry model will develop teacher learning communities that continually improve their instruction and student success. Although BASRC's model takes the school as the unit of change, its design calls for teachers to use inquiry practices in grade-level groups or subject departments and in the classroom to evaluate their instructional practice. Ideally, reform coordination occurs at multiple levels of the school, building communities of practice around key locations for teaching and learning.

BASRC's tools include a cycle of inquiry (COI) and an account-ability system with rubrics to assess school progress on culture change. The COI evolved into a six-step process for school-based inquiry: 1) use student assessment data to identify problems and provide an academic focus; 2) collect and analyze more data to refine the focus; 3) define measurable goals for teacher practice and student achievement; 4) build a work plan to implement changes at the school and at the grade or department level; 5) manage communication, shared leadership, assessment, and governance systems to support action; and 6) reflect on results and analyze them to determine what worked and to formulate next steps. The cycle continues as results define new problems for inquiry and change. The reform coordinator guides the faculty through this inquiry process and also brings knowledge and expertise into the school to support instructional changes to meet identified student needs.

One reform coordinator's work in a middle school new to BASRC illustrates how this role supports a school's use of inquiry to improve teaching and learning. By 2001, when this case study began, the coordinator had had 5 years of experience supporting the development of inquiry-based reform in a district elementary school that joined BASRC in 1996 (Paulsen Elementary, featured in chapter 2). She had considerable knowledge of the reform process, expertise in data analysis, and ideas about how to improve her facilitating role in schools new to BASRC.

The coordinator used a multistage strategy to engage the faculty in collaborative work and to support teachers' learning (see Coggins, 2005, for further detail). During the first stage, she worked with the principal to present data showing achievement gaps in literacy. She lobbied to get a majority vote to try out a literacy block (devoting extended instructional time to reading and writing) for low-performing students the following year. According to her plan, the teachers would use student performance data to assess the effectiveness of the intervention and refine it, thus establishing the school's first cycle of inquiry. Although a group of teachers actively opposed the intervention and others were skeptical, they were concerned about the achievement gaps revealed by the school data and agreed to give it a try.

The second stage began at the start of the next year. Assessment data showed significant improvement for the students involved in the intervention, but not enough to bring them up to grade level in another year or two. At this point, the reform coordinator helped define the need to develop the faculty's expertise in literacy. She enrolled a group of teachers in intensive off-site training through a secondary literacy support network, and these teachers formed a literacy task force that met weekly during the year. They became an effective leadership team, with the coordinator, for the next stage of school community-building. The team conducted a survey to assess teachers' perceptions and concerns about change and also reviewed their school's test data in relation to academic research on literacy. They planned to develop a comprehensive and radical proposal for change.

A third stage of school community-building began in the spring, when the team presented results of their research and analysis to the faculty. Team members walked the staff through the cycle of inquiry that linked patterns in students' performance to research on literacy teaching. They acknowledged and discussed staff concerns about change, and then presented a radical restructuring proposal for the next round of instructional change that addressed problems revealed by the assessment data. Because the coaches and teacher leaders presented a powerful, evidence-based case to their colleagues on the importance of radical change in addressing their students' literacy deficiencies, the faculty responded enthusiastically. Teachers agreed, "We can't stop doing this!" They voted to restructure the school day to support the intensive literacy instruction with underperforming students. Teachers who were previously reluctant to acknowledge that student achievement gaps could be closed were converted by the evidence at hand. They had become convinced of the need for change, and they saw the value of data-based inquiry as the process for school improvement.

The middle-school reform coordinator was a key agent in developing teacher leadership for schoolwide community practice. As a district employee and reputable educator in the region, she had the authority and respect needed to convene teachers who were committed to moving forward on an agenda for inquiry-based reform and to broker their access to professional knowledge and networks outside the school. By distributing leadership for inquiry-based reform throughout the school, she built broader school commitment and involvement. She helped institutionalize the reform practices. Further, she mediated relationships between the school, the district central office, and other schools involved in BASRC, serving as coordinator of the system's reform work.

Particularly when teacher community practice focuses on assessment data, schools depend upon the central office to support them with high-quality data systems and technical assistance in analyzing and interpreting disaggregated student data. This reform coordinator helped to build this district's capacity to provide these supports. She spanned boundaries between the school and the district central office, and between the school and professional networks outside the district, to broker resources for the development and learning of the school community.

Students as Entry

Intensive focus on individual students' work offers another strategy for developing teacher learning communities. By analyzing student work with colleagues, teachers deepen their understanding of individual learners in their classroom and how to better support their growth. They also learn to assess their teaching in terms of students' learning in a discipline and to provide effective feedback to their students.

Looking at an individual student's work in a teacher group can be a particularly powerful vehicle for developing a teacher learning community. Because the focus is on a particular student's learning, rather than directly on teaching, it provides a safe entry to collaborative practice. Also, it builds upon teachers' shared professional commitments to serving their students and connects with their interest in particular students in their classroom. Various protocols to support this process have developed over recent decades (see MacDonald et al., 2003). The protocol focuses teachers' inquiry and discourse on students and thus develops their clinical diagnostic skills, just as physicians' joint consultation around an individual patient case helps them to make professional judgments about care and develop shared standards of practice. As teachers discuss their students' work, they may invent new ways to assess student learning, as well as ways to improve instruction for individual students. Further, examining student work may open the door to new collegial discussions about norms and ethics of teaching. In particular, it brings into focus the whole child and the learning needs of students who struggle most in traditional school settings. This work can develop a stronger service ethic in the school community and strengthen teachers' commitments to serving all students.

One community facilitator working with the New York City school involved in the SATC initiative established a cross-discipline study group to look at student work, aiming to develop teachers' clinical expertise in supporting the whole child and to build a teacher community across the school. The ETN co-director who led this work told us that she "created a space with the help of the teachers where people can talk about their work. And therefore other people can be influenced by their work." Involvement in the group was voluntary, so teachers who opted in were ready to engage in dialogue with colleagues and a new kind of collaborative practices.

The study group used a number of Pat Carini's descriptive processes to look closely at student work and promote reflection among teachers about processes and supports of individual student learning (see Carini, 1993, for information about these processes). Over 4 years, the study group took on a variety of projects, including analysis of homework assignments and of the ways in which gender shaped students' work and social interactions. One aspect of the group's work involved each teacher bringing one student's work to the group for review. In each session, one student was the focus of review, and teachers typically brought several examples of that student's work. The review process consisted of several rounds of description and questions about the work, with the facilitator guiding the process so that each round built upon knowledge developed in the previous round. These reviews were designed not to be evaluative, but rather to focus on the child through his or her work. The process developed teachers' ability to see and appreciate each of their students and to customize instruction to build on individual knowledge, interests, culture, and personality.

Teachers' work together across disciplines broadened and deepened school norms of reflection. It enhanced the learning of teachers who worked in math teams with the school's NYCMP consultant, helping them to "look at chunks of our teaching, at our practice, to bring in an activity that we will share and talk about," in one teacher's words. Further, the study groups developed teacher leadership and capacity to sustain aspects of the student review process on their own with groups of colleagues.

Subject Discipline as Entry

Beginning the community development process through a subject discipline engages teachers in learning content more deeply, as well as understanding how to better support student learning in the subject. Through participation in a teacher community focused on subject instruction, teachers' professional identities shift toward that of an educator in the subject (see Stein, Silver, & Smith, 1998, for discussion of professional identity changes that evolve through math teachers' work as a community). Over time, teachers come to see themselves as members of subject professional communities within and beyond their schools.

The NYCMP consultant worked with math teachers at both grade levels and across the grades in the New York City middle school. With grade-level teams she worked on particular content and instructional challenges presented by their Connected Math Program (CMP) curriculum; with the school community of math teachers she worked on cross-cutting instructional issues, such as how to use student journals to assess their learning in mathematics. Beyond her work with teacher communities in the school, this consultant provided classroom coaching to teachers at their request and also taught a course at Lehman College that involved some of the teachers.

To begin the development of math teacher communities in the school, the consultant asked teachers to use CMP curriculum units in the same order so that they would share a math curriculum context for their study group discussions. Up until this point, the teachers differed in their ordering and coverage of particular CMP units. With a common focus on particular CMP units, teachers could share information about what instructional practices had gone well and what difficulties they encountered while teaching the lesson. Through dialogue about the lesson, they developed knowledge of how to better support students' learning of key concepts. As one math teacher put it:

> [The community] has been a source of support, to know that there are other people doing this. And to know, for example, that [another teacher] is moving into "Accentuate the Negative." So as she goes through this particular unit with her students, I can have conversations with her about what did and did not work with her class, and what I did in my lessons, so that she can give me advice for the future.

The consultant's role in building a math learning community in the school went beyond establishing a structure and curriculum for teachers' collaborative work. She supported their learning by framing questions for discussion among grade-level teams and among the entire math faculty. She accessed individual teachers' knowledge and provided personalized support, giving feedback and modeling reflective professional practice. In these ways, she established a learning environment for the teachers that was centered on mathematics instruction, teacher learners, assessment of teacher learning, and professional community. Math communities of practice developed as teachers discussed and designed lessons, and later assessed how these lessons affected student learning. As one teacher put it: "I would say that [the math teachers] have a reflective practice in that they not only reflect on students' strengths and challenges, but they also reflect on how to capitalize on those students' strengths."

Classroom coaching became an integral part of the NYCMP consultant's work to build a teacher community and to support change in math instruction in this school. By moving her work with teachers into the classroom, the consultant bridged boundaries between individual practice and group learning. She supported teachers in their efforts to translate new ideas and plans for math instruction into practice and helped them to open their classrooms and teaching to observation and critique by a colleague.

This consultant's work with a sixth-grade math teacher revealed the conditions and processes of skilled classroom coaching that support teacher community development and improved instruction. This coaching relationship began when the teacher invited her into her classroom, at a time when trust had developed through their work together in a school math team and the off-site course. As in her work with the teacher community, this consultant established the key principles of an effective learning environment in her classroom coaching relationship with a teacher—one that is a content-centered, learner-centered, assessment-centered, and community-centered environment for teacher learning.

The content of the coaching relationship centered on the dynamics of math teaching and learning with particular students—how did students respond to a lesson designed by the teacher or her math team? One important way in which this consultant worked to advance a teacher's understandings of effective math instruction was to co-teach a lesson. This was powerful because the teacher could see her own students respond to highly skilled math instruction. Further, the consultant modeled how a principle for math instruction that they were discussing in the school math team meetings or off-site class translates into classroom practices. For example, a teacher commented on how watching the consultant teach showed her the power of asking questions to prompt students' mathematical understandings:

> I think one main impact of [the consultant's] presence in our math class is her style of questioning. Her questioning motivates the students to think about what they are doing—the process. For example, when [a student] gives an answer, [the consultant] will ask him how . . . he got his answer. The open-ended questions she asked aid

all of my students to become more aware of their thinking in math.

Not only did this teacher develop a concrete vision of what her classroom could look like, her students became accustomed to a different kind of teaching and learning and could support their teacher's change.

The consultant also used intensive focus on one student learner in the class as a springboard to help teachers rethink their instruction. During the 2nd year of her work with the sixth-grade teacher, the consultant spent much of her time following one student, Miguel. He had found some success in the math class, but struggled in other subjects. To figure out why Miguel's experiences varied so greatly across his classes, the consultant observed him throughout the day, talked with each of his teachers, looked at his test scores and samples of his work, and worked with him on math problems. She shared her observation that Miguel became quickly bored with basic, repetitive tasks but thrived when engaged in higher-order problem-solving and discussing strategies in all subjects. When the teacher customized her math instruction for the student accordingly, his achievement soared. This experience enhanced her inclination and ability to work with all students as individual learners. She commented on her shift toward more learner-centered practice:

> From [the consultant] I've learned to listen to students' ideas. I've learned to understand that . . . students make connections and construct their learning at different rates. And if today we were talking about algebraic expressions [a student may] come up to me two weeks from now and say, "Ms. Eaton! Now I know what you were doing with algebraic expressions."

This consultant's coaching was learner-centered, in that her knowledge of the teacher as learner guided her decisions about how to facilitate change in her math instruction. For example, seeing this math teacher as having an "inquiry-based classroom," the consultant pushed her to deepen her questioning. (In contrast, her coaching with another teacher in the school focused on establishing classroom norms where students would talk as a whole class). The consultant described her effort to help the teacher learn to make connections between a student's knowledge and skills and questions that would advance his or her learning:

> We've looked at the way [one student] works in groups, the way he works alone, and the way he works as part of a whole class setting.

And we've looked at his work in all those areas, and then she and I worked together on her questioning [with this student] and how she follows it through. . . . We've focused a lot on the questioning and the sharing because that's where the learning [for her] really takes place.

In her community facilitation and coaching in the New York City middle school, this consultant established an assessment-centered learning environment for teachers. She provided feedback in the course of her work with the math teams and helped them to develop their capacity for reflection in instruction. She introduced practices and tools to scaffold teachers' learning of skills and habits of reflection and ongoing self-assessment in instruction. The teachers' capacity for reflective math teaching developed through weekly meetings with this consultant and keeping a journal on their math teaching.

Weekly meetings with individual teachers focused on a particular lesson and involved working through math problems the teacher proposed for the coming week, with the consultant raising questions and offering knowledge about how students might respond to the problems. This process scaffolded the teacher's planning and reflection on student learning. The sixth-grade math teacher commented, "I can anticipate questions, I can anticipate areas that might be difficult, I can anticipate extensions . . . how to take those students who grasp it and get done real quickly [and] pose additional problems so they can take it a step further." In keeping a journal, the teacher recorded her thoughts about lessons and her insights about individual students; she looked back on her journal entries to help her think through ways to strengthen her lessons and to better support her students' learning. Eventually these reflective practices became part of this teacher's daily work to support her learning when the consultant was gone.

Finally, the consultant created a community-centered learning environment in her coaching of this teacher and her colleagues. She worked with the teacher to determine the shape and focus of their work together in the classroom. The roles she assumed of observing, modeling, co-planning, and in-depth work with individual students laid the groundwork for the teacher's learning to change her instruction.

The sixth-grade teacher described how she learned to improve her teaching through collaboration with the math education consultant:

She was patient with my skepticism, and through her mentoring she created situations for me to experience trusting my students.

Her careful guidance on setting up my classroom, use of manipulatives, questioning techniques, and the use of journals set the stage for students to begin constructing their own learning.

Benefits for her sixth-grade students are apparent in this boy's response to our question: "What stands out for you about your math class?" He beamed and told us, with wide eyes:

Well, I really like it because we start out with a topic. Then we come up with a whole different math lesson, just like the one little problem that we were doing. It keeps getting bigger and bigger, and the kids they start talking about the different things that they saw, different patterns, different strategies, everything like that. And then you know that everybody's learning. It's not just all boring lesson, just open a textbook and start writing. It's like you work things out and you make grids and graphs and stuff to understand it better. And then you show it. And sometimes we put it on the overhead projector so people could see. You see [that] everybody's learning because kids talk about what they learn.

Through this teacher's efforts to improve her math teaching, and the skilled support the NYCMP consultant provided, a whole new world of mathematics opened up for this student and his classmates.

Facilitators played a key role in starting the development of teacher learning communities in these Bay Area and New York City schools. They brought knowledge and tools to focus teachers' joint work—around assessment data, students, and subject instruction. They established environments for teacher learning communities that were grounded in principles of learning. The professional norms of reflection and collaboration that they fostered over 3 to 4 years represent significant change in the teaching culture and should sustain improvement efforts into the future. The service ethic that developed through intense focus on individual students should sustain teachers' raised expectations for all students' achievement in the schools. Despite such positive outcomes, these cases of teacher community-building also reveal challenges for changing the professional cultures of schools.

Our up-close look at the facilitator's role in developing teacher learning communities has ignored school context conditions that supported or inhibited change, particularly school leadership. School administrators' active support of teacher community development and of the facilitator's role in the change process was particularly important. Schools where work on community-building did not get off the ground were those with weak or obstructive principals. Schools where tensions developed between teacher learning communities and other teachers in a school were stymied in their reform efforts when school administrators did not act to mediate the conflict. This was the case in the NYC middle school, where teacher involvement in collaborative work had been voluntary. Outsiders can only go so far to bridge competing school cultures and develop an inclusive school learning community.

SCHOOL LEADERSHIP FOR DEVELOPING TEACHER LEARNING COMMUNITIES

Because of their positional authority and control over school resources, principals are in a strategic position to promote or inhibit the development of a teacher learning community in their school. Administrators who use their authority to build a teacher community convey new expectations for teachers' work in the school, and they ensure that teachers have the time, space, and knowledge resources needed for collaborative work. They build trust and open communication among all teachers in the school. Conversely, administrators can limit change by not being proactive in these ways, or even undermine change by enforcing norms and routines of teachers' private practice.

In their effort to build teacher communities of practice across a school, principals and other school leaders face the challenges of

- Leveraging teacher commitment and support for collaboration
- Brokering or developing learning resources for teacher communities
- Supporting transitions between stages of community development.

Community facilitators from inside or outside the school system are key resources for addressing these challenges, but school administrators set the stage and conditions for starting and sustaining the community development process.

Leveraging Teacher Commitment and Support for Collaboration

School leaders play an important role in focusing the school on a pressing educational problem that sets the agenda for teacher collaboration and shared accountability for improvement. One way in which they can do this is by using student assessment data to highlight gaps in achievement for particular student groups and/or to identify a subject area or grade level in which students are generally performing poorly. For example, San Lucio's math department was propelled into its collaborative improvement effort by school data showing weak student engagement and performance in this subject. In BASRC schools, principals must become involved in the process of identifying foci for school improvement revealed through analysis of student achievement data.

Principals and other school leaders keep an eye out for opportunities to further encourage and support teacher learning to improve instruction. Most important, they locate a facilitator skilled in building communities of practice around an instructional focus that matches the school's identified needs. In the case of some SATC schools, the principals had previously contracted with the professional development organizations to work with teachers in the school, so the benefits of these principals' reform leadership were multiplied through the grant. Similarly, BASRC schools rely upon principals to take a leadership role in identifying gaps and problems for change revealed by student assessment data. The important role of school administrators in launching the school change process can be overlooked when the facilitator is the primary agent working with teacher communities. Both are essential to initiating and sustaining the change process.

Brokering Knowledge Resources for Teacher Communities

School administrators ideally work with facilitators and teachers to identify learning resources for teacher community improvement efforts. As teacher communities develop knowledge for improving their practice, they identify new directions for their learning and change. This kind of administrative support is therefore dynamic and evolving. For example, as the Bay Area middle school teachers developed expertise in evaluating their teaching through student assessment data, they focused their learning needs on literacy instruction. They brought literacy experts into the school, with the principal's encouragement and authorization. Principals support the development of teacher learning communities by tuning into and supporting successive learning frontiers of the teacher communities in the school.

Ideally, school administrators are proactive in getting the knowledge resources teacher communities need to improve their practice continually. Principals might broker relationships with local professional development organizations, intermediary reform organizations (e.g., BASRC), universities, or teacher networks that have solid reputations for high-quality support for teacher learning. Because they control professional development resources and other discretionary funds and have authority to negotiate the school's relationships with outside agents, principals effectively mediate teachers' access to such learning resources outside the school. In schools where the principal is not attuned to teachers' improvement efforts or is uninformed about local knowledge resources, teacher communities have weak learning opportunities. Conversely, a principal engaged in teacher community work and well connected to district specialists and to organizations with a strong track record in teacher professional development plays a key role in brokering resources that teachers need to sustain instructional improvement in the school.

Supporting Normative Transitions of Teacher Community

In addition to leveraging the start of teacher work to improve instruction and brokering knowledge resources for teacher community learning, school leaders play a central role in establishing school norms for community development. Analysts of school reform routinely observe that principal leadership is essential to serious changes in the culture and structure of schools. One reason is that teachers avoid taking the risks of exposing or changing their practice when they fear negative evaluations. The principal then must shift expectations for professional responsibility and instructional quality from the individual teacher to the school in order to define the teacher group as the accountable unit. The principal's role in supporting normative change for a teacher learning community goes well beyond no-harm assurances, however. Given the developmental nature of building teacher communities, principals have particular roles to play during the novice, intermediate, and advanced stage of community development. Although we have focused on the beginning stage of community-building thus far in this chapter, analysis of the principal's role in developing a teacher learning community necessarily considers the problem of transitions between community stages.

Reflecting on their own experiences as principals developing school learning communities, Nancy Mohr and Alan Dichter (2001) offer a useful analysis of the particular roles that a school administrator plays to support the faculty's transition between stages. During what we refer to as the novice stage of community development, change focuses on building social trust and norms for group decision-making. To support normative change, the administrator takes a strong role in designing community work (or authorizing and supporting a facilitator to do so). Then, as conflicts inevitably arise within the group, the principal surfaces differences in beliefs that underlie conflict and establishes norms for problem-solving around controversies.

Mohr and Dichter argue that teachers' trust of school authority figures is key to moving beyond this initial stage of community-building, since the faculty inevitably confronts the limits of democratic decision-making. The principal must be clear about what decisions remain in the administrative purview, while emphasizing a high priority for teacher learning in communities and collective responsibility among teachers across the school. By modeling and teaching inclusiveness and the role of mutual consultation in community practice, school administrators can avoid the oft-observed development of a schism between innovative and traditional teaching cultures in the school.

At the intermediate stage of learning community development, challenges center on sustaining collaborative work when the payoffs are uncertain and the faculty fears that its work is unproductive. During this stage, a principal moves the community forward by (a) promoting risk-taking by acknowledging that failure is a natural part of change, (b) ensuring that the community has the expertise and support to critically analyze its practice, and (c) supporting its move to public accountability and comfort through reflection on its practices.

Once an advanced or mature school learning community has developed, the principal's role shifts to sustaining the community and its work. While celebrating the habits and norms developed for assessing and improving teaching and learning, the administrator keeps the faculty from becoming complacent over its successes and continues to focus on the shortfall between expectations for students' learning and actual accomplishment as assessed by a variety of measures. Also, the principal and other school leaders work to institutionalize the routines, tools, and resources that support community collaboration and learning.

Significantly, many schools involved in initiatives that aim to develop teacher learning communities do not move from the novice to the intermediate stage, and most do not transition to an advanced stage after several years. They become stuck in a stage of collaborative work that falls short of teacher learning community practice. This reality highlights the need for clearer understanding of the problem of change. The stagnated development of teacher community stems from weak leadership for change among school administrators, reflecting their limited opportunities to learn how to be effective in these roles. It also testifies to the complex challenges entailed in developing teacher learning communities widely in U.S. schools.

TENSIONS AND CHALLENGES IN CHANGING SCHOOL CULTURE

School leaders confront tensions and trade-offs in designing strategies to develop teacher learning communities. For one, in drawing boundaries for school community development, leaders weigh *competing values of voluntarism and inclusiveness.* The cases in this chapter point to trade-offs between inviting teacher participation in voluntary collaborative work versus requiring teachers to participate in collaborative work at the school or grade/department level.

Voluntarism has clear benefits and risks. On one hand, teachers' collaborative work can deepen more quickly in voluntary groups, and learning can be enhanced through additional voluntary off-site professional development. On the other hand, professional disagreements and gaps in learning opportunities between the voluntary teacher community and the rest of the faculty are likely to grow, as they did in the New York City school discussed earlier in this chapter (see also Gamoran et al., 2003).

Entry with the whole school faculty also has benefits and costs. On the plus side, a subculture strongly opposed to change is less likely to grow. Differences in instructional philosophy among teachers can be engaged in ways that deepen discourse and learning in teacher communities (Achinstein, 2002). On the other hand, involving entire school faculties in required collaboration risks the possibility that teachers will enter the work with a project mentality, regarding the work as "contrived collegiality" disconnected from their professional practice (Hargreaves, 1991). This mentality ensures that organizational change will not move beyond rituals of collaborative practice to meaningful joint work to improve teaching and learning, i.e., will not move from single-loop to double-loop learning (Argyris, 1982). This outcome was quite common among BASRC schools as described in chapter 2. If a whole school strategy for building teacher community is to succeed, it requires the kind of shared leadership and expert facilitation that moved the Bay Area middle school toward a community of practice in a relatively short time.

Similarly, school leaders face a *tension between recruiting teachers who place priority on collaboration with colleagues versus bringing veteran teachers into new norms of collaborative practice.* A teacher selection strategy is clearly desirable from the school administrator and teacher community standpoint. Screening teachers on their interest in collaborative practice brings capacity for change into the school and may create a critical mass of teachers to form a teacher learning community. As noted in chapter 2, the San Lucio math department sustained its collaborative professional practice partly by attracting beginning math teachers who prefer this mode of professional practice. In schools where many teachers oppose collaboration, reform leaders face an uphill struggle to build communities of practice, and administrators who are strong community leaders may seek positions in schools and districts where their mission has more support.

Teachers' *collective bargaining agreements pose different, particular challenges for school community-building.* Local teacher organizations' contracts and leadership more or less constrain the use of teacher selection to develop school learning community and, more generally, the ability of school administrators to establish conditions of teachers' work that support collaborative practice. Collective bargaining agreements generally limit potential for free hiring practices, but they vary widely in the opportunities and constraints they set for teacher learning communities. Some union locals, such as those involved in the Teacher Union Reform Network (TURN), have been proactive in setting policy to support the development of teacher learning communities. In such districts, principals and other system leaders ideally work with union leaders to implement the enabling conditions for school change, but this requires them to break the conventional frame of union–district contention. In districts where union contracts and leaders place strong limits on teacher collaboration beyond classroom contact requirements, school leaders face the challenge of interpreting and acting on the policies in ways that protect teachers but also move the school change agenda forward.

Other challenges and trade-offs in building teacher community arise from *multiple levels of practice in a school*—including grade levels in elementary schools and subject matter departments in secondary schools. Teachers in these units share instructional contexts—student developmental stages and academic content and curriculum. These are natural settings for teacher community work to improve instruction, and assessment data often reveal disparities in student performance between them. Yet investing in community facilitation at all of these levels and across all content areas is impractical, and school leaders face the considerable challenge of synchronizing teacher community development at the school level and in these subcommunities.

Further complicating the picture is evidence that these school units often differ widely in the strength and character of their teacher communities. For example, the math department featured in chapter 2 was an island of collaborative practice in San Lucio High School. The particular problems of change, and the leadership and learning needs of teacher subcommunities, are likely to vary widely within schools. Some teaching units may need help developing trust and addressing conflict constructively, while others need help exploiting networks and knowledge resources to refine their improvement efforts. While high schools pose the greatest challenge because of organizational complexity, no school is monolithic in terms of the strength and character of teacher subcommunities responsible for students at a particular grade level or in a particular subject.

School and district leaders sometimes perceive a *trade-off between pursuing the goal of building a teacher learning community and responding to accountability pressures from external policy systems.* Norms of collective responsibility and collaborative teaching practice develop slowly, yet high-stakes accountability systems demand fast, significant improvement in student achievement. The press for immediate gains in test scores pushes a pace of change that can undermine the development of school learning communities. Many BASRC schools working to move their schools out of "underperforming" status, for example, were distracted from their agenda to develop collective responsibility for improving student achievement. Schools' efforts to boost scores quickly worked against community development and innovation when they turned the spotlight on individual teachers' classroom outcomes and emphasized curriculum implementation as the primary reform strategy.

Pressures associated with high-stakes accountability systems generate other trade-offs for school leaders. Exploring new instructional practices leads to powerful forms of learning for teachers as they come to understand connections between particular classroom innovations and students' learning. Yet this experimental approach may sacrifice a short-term boost in performance. A community of practice preoccupied with test scores may elect to stick with known practices and make the most of them, rather than to experiment with new ones. Leaders are challenged to find a balance that protects the community from the consequences of failure, but also furthers experimentation and the use of data to evaluate change. Organizational theorist James March (1991) terms this tension the "exploration/exploitation trade-off" and sees the proper balance between them as a primary element in system survival and success.

A related issue for school leaders is managing disappointing outcomes. A community learns through examining the mismatch between goals and performance—that is, they confront the "brutal facts" about student learning in their school (Schön, 1983). However, candid description and discussion of shortfalls in student learning can trigger angry responses from parents and community. This anger erodes teachers' willingness to highlight disappointments as well as celebrate successes. Making failure public presented an ongoing challenge for BASRC schools as they worked through inquiry cycles.

Finally, schools and districts face *trade-offs in allocating the professional development resources they control*. While investing in a community facilitator is essential for developing teacher communities of practice, other kinds of professional development opportunities are also central to teacher learning and instructional improvement. Classroom coaching is an important complement to teacher learning community work on content instruction, yet it is costly in terms of peer coaches' release time and the intensive professional development needed to ensure high-quality coaching. And as we describe in the next chapter, off-site courses and institutes provide particular kinds of support for the growth of a teacher learning community and knowledge resources for the community's ongoing learning to improve teaching practice.

4

Professional Development in Support of Teacher Learning Communities

Teacher communities that stay within the walls of their school, like teachers who close their classroom door to colleagues, shut out the knowledge resources and collegial support essential to learning and change. Insulation from broader professional networks will stymie the improvement efforts of even the most engaged and collaborative teacher community. Without a flow of new knowledge and tools for effective instruction, a teacher community is dependent solely upon its members for solving problems of practice; such insular communities eventually use up their knowledge and energy resources. Further, off-site professional development affords particular kinds of learning opportunities that school communities cannot provide readily—especially the chance to be a learner in a subject discipline, to experience high-quality instruction, and to "break set" in conceptual understandings of teaching and learning (Putnam & Borko, 2000). By getting outside of their classrooms and teaching role, teachers who participate in high-quality courses and institutes are able to rethink their practice and bring fresh perspectives on instruction to their school communities. Here we argue that teacher communities' ability to make significant improvements in instruction and student achievement depends upon teachers' involvement in multiple professional development venues and learning opportunities, within and beyond the school.

Evidence that school-based teacher learning communities are key to improving student achievement could be interpreted to mean that districts and schools should no longer invest in off-site professional development for teachers. To the contrary, teacher professional development through courses, institutes, and networks contributes important and unique resources for school communities' learning and change.

However, the value of off-site professional development to teacher learning and instructional improvement is highly conditional. What teachers call "sit-'n-git" workshops do little to advance teaching quality (Smylie, 1994). In such professional development venues, where speakers have little if any dialogue with teachers in the audience, connections between transmitted knowledge and the learning needs of the teacher are loose and uncertain. In contrast, a course or institute that creates an effective learning environment for teachers can be a powerful context for teacher learning and a catalyst and support for instructional improvement in a teacher community.

This chapter highlights the unique and important contributions that off-site professional development makes to teacher learning and improved instruction, illustrates how high-quality instruction in a university course and a district-sponsored summer practicum makes a difference for school communities, and considers implications for the design of professional development systems to build and sustain teacher learning communities.

SPECIAL CONTRIBUTIONS OF
OFF-SITE PROFESSIONAL DEVELOPMENT

Off-site professional development makes particular contributions to teacher learning and ability to improve instruction, contributions valuable to school-based teacher communities across the developmental spectrum. Although strong school communities are better able to take advantage of off-site learning opportunities—even making use of one-shot workshops to expand their repertoire of skills and practices—teachers in both weak and strong school communities benefit from intensive, sustained professional development focused on content instruction (Cohen & Hill, 2001). High-quality off-site professional development affords teachers unique opportunities to access knowledge for content instruction, to rethink their practice, and to experience learning in a community of peers.

Knowledge Resources for Teacher Learning Communities

The importance of off-site professional development and networks for teacher community learning and improvement is readily seen in the practices of advanced learning communities like San Lucio High School's math department. In these communities, teachers' focused work to improve instruction and their reflections on innovations prompt them to search for particular kinds of knowledge and exemplars. For example, the math department strategically sought information and support for its detracking efforts and consulted regularly with a local math educator who is skilled in teaching heterogeneous math classes. More generally, interaction with math colleagues outside the school in regional professional associations and informal local networks ensures that the community stays up to date on research-based knowledge for math instruction.

Courses and institutes focused on subject content and content instruction enable teachers to deepen their knowledge for teaching, offering systematic and sustained inquiry into subject matter of the sort that facilitators working with school communities cannot provide. As teachers develop new knowledge off-site, individually or as a school team, their ability to contribute to their school communities' learning and improvement efforts is enhanced. A teacher community's learning depends upon the knowledge and skills of its members and upon its ongoing access to knowledge resources for teaching.

Opportunities to Rethink Teaching Practice

Off-site professional development supports additional kinds of teacher learning that are difficult to achieve through facilitated work in school-based teacher communities. In particular, courses and institutes support teachers to take the role and perspective of a learner in a subject area and afford them the chance to experience high-quality instruction. These learning opportunities enable teachers to rethink teaching in ways that support their efforts to improve instruction in their classroom and their ability to lead change in their school community.

Taking the role of learner in a subject area prompts teachers to consider how and how well their students' learning is supported in the classroom. This shift in perspective is extremely difficult to accomplish in the school setting, where teachers are in their identity and routines of being an educator. In their school, teachers also feel responsible to know the subject matter they teach and are less comfortable acknowledging the limitations of their knowledge. In a supportive instructional environment away from their school, teachers are freed up to be learners in a subject discipline and thus can develop new understandings of content learning, as well as new knowledge of content. Sustained professional development in a discipline affords teachers the opportunity to make conceptual shifts in their understandings of subject instruction (see Lieberman & Wood, 2003, for a discussion of teacher change through the National Writing Project institutes).

Further, in experiencing high-quality instruction as a learner, teachers come to understand the principles and practices of an effective learning environment. The teacher educator or professional developer who leads teacher learning provides models of teaching in these environments. As teachers reflect on the instructional conditions and processes that support their own learning, they draw connections to their teaching and imagine new ways of supporting student learning in their classroom. They are prompted to reflect on the assumptions and routines of their instructional practice and to more or less fundamentally reconceptualize teaching and learning in their classroom. For example, teachers who for the first time experience powerful learning through discourse with peers around discipline practice—such as solving a math problem or writing a short story—are motivated to try to establish learning communities for students in their classrooms.

Scaffolds for Teacher Learning Communities

When teachers are part of a learning community created in a course or other professional development venue, they come to appreciate the process and potential for learning with other teachers. This experience makes them more open to the development of professional learning communities with school colleagues and may even prompt them to become leaders in changing their school's culture. Weak school communities have the most to gain from this particular learning opportunity provided by off-site professional development, since teachers who participate in school-based learning communities will have already learned community practices and benefits.

Some kinds of off-site professional development offer teachers the opportunity to observe how educators collaborate to design, implement, and evaluate instruction. The experienced teacher educators who lead a summer institute, for example, model reflective collaborative practice for participants. They might even bring teacher participants into planning and leading roles. This kind of learning can prompt and guide teachers' work with school colleagues to design and provide high-quality instruction for their students.

In some instances, off-site professional development takes as its focus the development of collaborative teacher communities. Although school-based facilitation of teacher learning community development is essential for changing school culture, a multiday workshop or school retreat can provide teachers with conceptual frameworks, organizational designs, and tools that scaffold the change process. For example, teachers in a high school School Learning Community (SLC) we studied participated in a weeklong summer workshop called Interdisciplinary Teaming Experience. The workshop supported teams to develop norms and goals for collaboration and to design protocols for their work together over the year. This established crucial grounding for the team's development as a learning community during its 1st year, since none of the teachers had prior experience working closely with colleagues. Beyond the benefits of its community-building curriculum and resources, this off-site workshop gave teacher teams the chance to be together for a sustained period of time; they got to know one another personally and developed consensus about individuals' strengths that the team would draw upon (Eilers, Vagle, & Talbert, 2004).

QUALITY PROFESSIONAL DEVELOPMENT AND ITS VALUE TO TEACHER LEARNING COMMUNITIES

Locating off-site professional development away from the demands and constraints of teachers' daily work lives does not guarantee a powerful learning experience. The typical teacher education course and one-shot district workshop that cast teachers in a passive learner role do not prompt teachers to learn new principles for instruction. But even when surface features of high-quality professional development are established—sustained over several days and involving school teams in collaborative work—the quality of learning depends upon the facilitators' expertise in teaching educators. For example, when a district implemented these design features in a new summer literacy institute but provided little professional development for the institute facilitators running the sessions, the quality of teaching and learning was highly uneven and quite shallow on the whole. Most teacher participants took away ideas for new practices but did not make the conceptual shifts needed for significant instructional improvement. In order to make the special contributions highlighted earlier, an institute or course must exemplify the principles of an effective learning environment, rather than merely establish their design features. For example, teachers can learn the value of a learning community for knowledge development only if the course or institute successfully creates one for them.

Our evidence regarding the nature and effectiveness of high-quality professional development comes primarily from observations of the Students at the Center (SATC) off-site courses and institutes. These professional development opportunities were exceptionally well designed and facilitated by highly skilled teacher educators. The case of a New York City Math Project (NYCMP) yearlong course illustrates how principles for a high-quality learning environment can be established in the traditional venue of a course for teachers. Further, it shows how teachers' course participation contributes to their school community. Philadelphia SATC's summer practicum exemplifies how learning principles can be infused in a summer institute designed collaboratively by a district and local professional organizations—the Philadelphia Writing Project and Philadelphia Education Fund, in this case—and how it builds school community. In both cases, the off-site professional development was designed to complement work in schools, and so the special contributions it makes to teacher learning come into focus.

As the cases illustrate, teachers who experience an effective learning environment come to see the dynamic interplay of principles for high-quality instruction—focus on content, attention to individual learners, and ongoing assessment in a learning community. They thus develop the conceptual understandings to ground their efforts to significantly improve instruction for the students in their classroom. We emphasize through these examples that the special contributions afforded by off-site professional development depend upon highly skilled professional development practice.

A Math Education Course as Vehicle for Teacher Learning and School Change

SATC teams provided teachers with multiple entry points for professional development, including courses, school-based projects and study groups, and classroom coaching. This design for their work with schools ensured broad faculty participation in at least one of the learning environments and created the potential for teachers to benefit from mutually reinforcing learning opportunities. While the on-site work built teacher communities and supported individual teachers as they reshaped their classroom practice, the off-site courses provided a place for teachers to explore disciplines and content learning in a high-quality learning environment.

In the NYCMP courses, which were offered as two semester-long courses each year for a period of 4 years, participants were both math *teachers* and math *learners*. The course content focused on how to establish an effective environment for mathematics learning. Class routines developed for the course exemplified this outcome. Course facilitators modeled effective practices, and teachers collaborated to solve math problems that were aligned with their CMP math curricula. Teachers then discussed the mathematics concepts and practices the facilitators used to develop teachers' new understandings. To help teachers connect their personal experiences as learners in the course with their students' experiences in their classrooms, facilitators prompted individual and group reflection through the use of journals (in which teachers reflected on their classroom practice relevant to foci of the course) and discussion. The reflections helped teachers understand how conditions of the NYCMP class environment promote learning in mathematics. Group discussions and collaboration on problem-solving forged collegial relationships within the class, which established the course as a safe place to explore new ideas and created a new professional community for teachers in the class.

Instructional routines in the math education class established conditions of an effective learning environment. The class environment was content-centered (a focus on math problem-solving), learner-centered (customized support of teacher learning from the instructor and facilitators), assessment-centered (use of journals for self-assessment and focus on links between teaching and learning), and community-centered (collaboration, discourse, and reflection among teachers in the class).

Teacher learning from these practices is evident in the experiences of the sixth-grade teacher in the New York City middle school featured in chapter 3's analysis of school-based facilitation of teacher communities development. This teacher participated in the off-site course, as well as in school study groups, math team meetings, and classroom coaching. Her reflections on what she learned through the course highlight its special learning opportunities for teachers.

Taking the Perspective of the Learner

This teacher commented that the experience of the NYCMP course changed her view of herself as a learner and teacher of mathematics. As a teacher who had stuck close to the text in math instruction, she had not developed a sense of herself as being competent in solving complex math problems. Rather, she closely followed the curriculum scripts and remembered herself as a mediocre math student. Through the course, she developed new math knowledge and confidence in her ability to explore mathematical concepts and strategies:

> At [the beginning of the first course] I felt very, very frustrated. . . . I can remember maybe one or two times when I sat in that class with other teachers, and I just looked down at my paper and was ready to burst into tears because I thought I understood how to solve a particular problem, and then I saw people get up and they had all these brilliant ideas, and I just felt so stupid. . . . I think a turning point for me was one week working out some problem. And as [the facilitators] walked around, they looked at me and said, "We want you to share how you did this." And I shared and there was a discussion generated by what I'd done and all of a sudden I felt validated.

This teacher goes on to say, "I began to see the transformation of my classroom to be a result of my own transformation—looking at myself as a math learner."

Being a learner in this off-site professional community influenced this teacher's thinking about teaching and learning and about mathematics in ways that directly influenced her classroom practice. For example, she created a learning environment that validated students' uses of multiple strategies, as this was an approach that she felt had greatly benefited her own learning in the course. During one class, for instance, she and her sixth-grade students discussed a variety of approaches to solving a homework problem. She concluded the class by showing how she solved the problem and saying, "See? It takes all different ways. . . . What works quickest in your head may not be what works quickest in my head. What you feel comfortable with may not be what I feel comfortable with. . . . It's what way is best for you." The teacher thus reproduced for her students the experience that she had in her NYCMP math education courses when she shared multiple problem-solving strategies in a learning community of peers.

Conceptual Change in Math Instruction

This teacher had little personal experience with high-quality learning environments prior to participating in the course. She had assumed that test-based, teacher-directed instruction was most effective, since this is how she had learned math in school and how she learned to teach math in her teacher education program. But as she saw how the design for teaching and learning in the course led to deeper knowledge of mathematics and of math teaching, she began to construct a new image of what her classroom could look like. She explained:

> What [the facilitator] will do is listen when she hears a conversation about a problem, when we're talking about math and strategies. . . . When we come together to discuss our strategies, she will bring those things out—things that we might have otherwise overlooked. She will remind us, "I heard you saying this and that, what made you think that way?" And then you realize that a) she was listening to you, b) there was value in what you were saying, and c) when it's shared with the entire group, other people are saying, "Oh, I never thought of that." or "I was thinking of that, too." And I think that provides a fantastic model for us in the classroom—that our questioning should be based on listening to students.

This teacher experienced several breakthroughs in conceptual understandings of math teaching and learning through the NYCMP course. Other teachers who participated in the course had similar experiences. One emphasized that it wasn't the SATC initiative or course design that mattered for her learning, but rather the quality of instruction in the course: "It's watching [the consultant] teach those math classes at Lehman and being able to be part of watching a real master teacher teach that matters." Through their example, the course facilitators showed teachers how all parts of an effective learning environment work together in daily, monthly, and yearly time frames.

Professional Community in the Off-site Course

The course also placed teachers within a community of colleagues, where they learned to value the role of discourse in learning. Describing how the course improved her teaching, the sixth-grade teacher commented on her access to the expert knowledge of the instructor and peers in the course:

> When something would come up [in my classroom] that I couldn't answer, I'd say, "I'm going to school tonight. I'll ask [the facilita-

tors] and the other teachers." . . . The next day, [the students would say], "Ms. Eaton, did you ask? Did you find out?" And it was so neat.

An example of this interaction occurred during a unit on fractions. One of her students, Marisa, asked, "Why is it when you multiply with fractions it seems like you're dividing?" Not sure of the answer herself, the teacher went to the next NYCMP class, during which participants were given a problem involving the use of pattern blocks to show multiplication of fractions. After working with another teacher to solve the problem, she consulted with one of the course facilitators about how they could modify it to answer Marisa's question. Through dialogue with outside experts, this teacher created a way to help Marisa use manipulatives such as pattern blocks to understand the multiplication of fractions. The students in her class came to see the NYCMP course as a resource for their own math learning.

Benefits to the School Learning Community

The NYCMP math education course and its facilitators became an important source of knowledge and expertise in mathematics and math education for faculty and students in the schools participating in SATC. The conceptual, mathematics-focused forum of the off-site course complemented the learning and support that teachers gained through working with math colleagues in grade-level and schoolwide math meetings. It provided these teachers with a concrete example of the standards for content instruction that they were working to establish for their students.

Further, as documented for the middle school math teacher we followed, the course provided powerful examples of how collegial discourse around mathematics problems and problems of math instruction develops individual understandings and shared knowledge among teachers. Learning to value colleagues as resources for improving one's practice strengthens teachers' interest and involvement in school-based community; it supports the shift in professional norms from private practice toward collaboration.

The off-site course also provided teachers with a place for investigating mathematics in a sustained way, and thus it accelerated teacher learning around mathematics instruction in the community. The participation of several teachers from each SATC school ensured that a critical mass of teachers were bringing new knowledge into the work of the math department and grade-level teams in their school.

Over 4 years, math teaching in the New York City middle school changed significantly through the NYCMP consultant's work with math teams and teachers in courses. One teacher told us:

> I just really feel like [the consultant] changed the whole culture of math and math instruction. There's a real unanimity among the staff here and really good math teachers. It's a good place to come and teach math. . . . I know it wasn't that way four years ago. The eighth graders that I had four years ago? It was very sad: incredibly, incredibly smart kids who by the eighth grade didn't have any concept of "percent." . . . It's nice to be [now] in a school where I feel like, in general, the kids are getting a good math education. And I feel like math is really important for kids who don't come from a high socioeconomic background. So it makes me feel really happy to be part of [this] school.

A Summer Practicum as a Vehicle for Teacher Learning and School Change

The SATC team of professional development organizations in Philadelphia included a 3-week summer practicum in its work with 32 schools in two of the district's clusters. The content focus of the Philadelphia Students at the Center (PSATC) practicum was on creating a learner-centered instructional environment and on the dynamics of effective classroom instruction. Involving students in this professional development thus was critical to PSATC's aims. The practicum design integrated classroom instruction and facilitator-guided teacher reflection and professional development.

The practicum was designed to build teachers' understanding of high-quality instruction through the experience of teaching students with ongoing facilitator guidance and feedback. Parents were included so that they would learn how to collaborate with teachers to enhance student learning in classrooms and to become part of their school's learning community.[1] The practicum design included 3 days of planning and professional development for participating teacher and parent teams, who formed small learning communities around an essential question and a theme, such as "The Rain Forest" or "What Is Multiculturalism?" During subsequent days, school teams worked in the mornings with groups of 15 to 20 students while facilitators observed their teaching and answered questions or modeled a technique when asked (facilitators were experienced teacher consultants from the Philadelphia Writing

Project and district cluster professional development staff). Afternoon sessions were devoted to debriefing, during which facilitators stretched participants' thinking by questioning their practices and how they would modify them for the next day. The practicum culminated with student exhibitions from each of the small learning communities.

The instructional design for teachers and parents featured a cycle of learning about high-quality instruction: putting knowledge into practice with the support of peers, reflecting on student responses and learning, and then refining practice based on this new knowledge. The student–adult ratio of about 3:1 made it possible for participants to focus closely on student learning in the context of class instruction, avoiding obstacles such as classroom management problems. Practicum designers hoped that this more ideal environment would support teachers to break set, i.e., experience instruction in radically new ways. Further, facilitators could offer immediate support when teachers felt uncomfortable taking risks.

The practicum design and practices exemplify how principles for high-quality learning environments for teachers can be established in this particular mode of off-site professional development. The quality of the environment hinged on the facilitators' skills in enacting these principles. Teacher leaders in the Philadelphia Writing Project were particularly well prepared for this work, having developed deep knowledge and skills for supporting peer learning through their sustained participation in Writing Project leadership development opportunities (see Lieberman & Wood, 2003). One teacher commented that the facilitators "were not just the classic person who comes in and doesn't really know anything, and you wonder how they got there. They basically were comfortable and constantly using [learner-centered teaching], even as they were talking to us and problem-solving."

The practicum focus on the dynamics of classroom instruction with students—or the interplay of students with content and assessments in a learning community—was intended to create a bridge between knowledge from courses and real classrooms. As the lead designer from the Philadelphia Education Fund put it:

> You can present material in an institute. And people enjoy the institute, but they really don't know that they don't understand or that they don't get it. . . . And so the practicum is that place where when they actually go in and try to do what you've been presenting. Then it's like, "Oh, is that what you meant? Is this what you're talking about?" . . . And there are the "aha!" moments when they

really see the power of what it is that you've been talking about. . . . In the institutes or [school-based] workshops, they never see the results. They never see it happen. . . . So the practicum is a way of just providing a lot of support. And they will try it because you have a small class size, you have a lot of adults who are there, you have a trusting environment.

Although we lack data on student achievement benefits from the PSATC practicum, many teachers and parents commented that it was "the best thing I've ever done." Teachers described how working in a classroom setting with constant feedback and support led them to rethink their conceptions of high-quality instruction. One teacher described an "aha!" moment when she saw what her students were capable of learning together, after a colleague who was co-teaching suggested that she give them more responsibility for designing their work.

The practicum, like the NYCMP math courses, provided teachers with personal experiences of learning in a high-quality instructional environment and gave them a reference point for reflecting on their own practice. In some cases, teachers changed their perceptions of their students' abilities and, in turn, their commitments to improving their learning. Several teachers reported that seeing substantial student progress over the 3 weeks of the practicum class had revamped their notions of what children in this extremely low-income community could achieve in an effective learning environment. Changed expectations for student learning reaffirmed the teachers' service ethic and thus enhanced professionalism in the schools.

Although nearly all participants in the summer practicum found it transformational, many had trouble bringing what they had learned back to their classrooms. One participant said, "Asking kids what they would do rather than telling them what to do is a lot harder with the whole class, especially when there's no one else [peer or facilitator] in the room." Although they had hoped to make big changes, most were only able to make incremental changes at best in their classroom practice.

Even such exemplary off-site professional development falls short of the goal of improving instruction. When we observed significant learning and change in teachers' classroom practice, it was among those teachers who had multiple reinforcing learning opportunities—facilitated work with colleagues in the school, coaching or peer feedback in the classroom, and off-site courses or institutes.

IMPLICATIONS FOR
TEACHER PROFESSIONAL DEVELOPMENT SYSTEMS

Our research on teacher learning to improve student achievement points to the mutually reinforcing character of different kinds and settings for professional development. Not only is the development of school learning communities essential to improving teaching quality and student achievement, but investing in high-quality off-site professional development is critical as well. While sometimes pitted against one another as alternative strategies for professional development, we believe that they are mutually reinforcing and should be considered essential components of a school or district agenda to improve student learning and close achievement gaps.

Professional development venues and practices described here aim to build strong and innovative professional communities in school. When carried out effectively, each offers unique learning opportunities to teachers. Together they create a powerful strategy for improving the quality of instruction in urban schools. A strategy of combining multiple approaches to supporting teacher learning builds upon three principles:

- *Complementarity.* Each mode of teacher professional development—facilitated work with teacher communities, classroom coaching, and off-site professional development—offers a unique kind of learning opportunity for teachers. School community facilitation focuses teachers on evidence of their students' performance and guides their collaboration to improve teaching and learning. Classroom coaching supports teachers' efforts to change instruction to meet diverse student needs, to translate learning from colleagues and courses into practice. Off-site professional development can provide teachers with new experiences and perspectives on learning and instruction as well as new collaborative relationships with parents. Each is critical to developing a school's capacity to improve student achievement. A system agenda to develop teacher learning communities across schools would invest in multiple venues and learning opportunities for teachers, provided that they all meet the quality standards illustrated here.
- *Interdependence.* The values of off-site professional development for improved instruction are conditioned by school norms of professionalism and teacher collaboration. Where communi-

ties of practice have developed in schools, teachers take advantage of a wide range of professional development opportunities that contribute to their ongoing learning and strengthen their community. This empirical observation, across several initiatives that we have documented over the past decade, points to the interdependence of school community conditions and, by implication, to the problem that inequalities in school capacity increase over time.

- *Synergy.* A strong hypothesis from our and others' research on school improvement efforts is that significant improvement in student achievement depends upon teachers participating in facilitated work of a school learning community, classroom coaching, and intensive off-site professional development. The schools and classrooms where improvements have been the greatest are those in which teachers have many supports for their ongoing learning and improvement.

Unfortunately, school demographics and prior school community conditions are strong predictors of teachers' and schools' participation in organized learning opportunities. Schools serving the poorest students and schools with the weakest professional communities were least involved in BASRC's work, for example (Center for Research on the Context of Teaching, 2002). This suggests that without intervention, off-site professional development will continue to serve teachers in the most advanced school communities.

Improving student achievement in U.S. schools requires developing the capacity of all schools to build teacher learning communities through skilled facilitation of teacher groups, classroom coaching, and high-quality professional development in off-site venues. This improvement agenda and strategy involves a significant shift of school and district resources toward professional development. It also requires a change in thinking about teacher quality—away from credentials and toward a notion of day-to-day resources that teachers draw upon to ensure high-quality instruction for students in their school. This challenge implicates a broad agenda for learning in the contexts of teaching.

5

Teacher Learning Communities and the Broader Context

This chapter moves outside the teachers' immediate community to consider how others in the broader context affect teachers' learning communities. We argue that even if resources to support teachers' professional growth were uniformly accessible, timely, and relevant, they would not be enough to sustain and deepen teachers' learning or the learning that occurs in site-based communities. Even the best-designed professional development resources will fall short, and the most robust professional community will dissolve, when other elements in teachers' professional context ignore, frustrate, or work at cross-purposes with the learning and change they intend.

Many in the district environment who have an interest in the quality and consequences of teachers' learning are uninformed about its most fundamental features and the learning communities that nurture it. Sustaining professional communities and deepening teachers' learning and ability to act upon it depend on a broader context. Specifically, they depend on outside players knowing about teachers' learning goals and needs, and their capacity and inclination to support teachers' efforts and learning communities in material and moral terms. For teachers' knowledge to deepen, for their learning communities to become more sophisticated and rigorous, various people inside and outside the school and the school system must understand its purpose, believe in it, and support the classroom practices associated with it. Who are these actors, and how do they matter to teachers' learning and professional community?

SYSTEM ADMINISTRATORS

Don't forsake the administrator. If you want teachers to really get involved in learning, get the administrator involved first.
—Philadelphia middle school principal

Administrators' attitudes and actions are critical to whether and what teachers learn, as well as how much teachers' learning turns into productive, sustainable classroom practices. By direction and indirection, administrators communicate priorities for teachers' work, establish norms around professional development and accountability, and create a climate that fosters or dampens teachers' willingness to engage in candid reflection and challenging inquiry. At both school and district levels, administrative tasks essential to teachers' learning and learning communities include building a shared vision and common language about practice; convening and supporting reflective conversations, using evidence and data about student learning; and establishing norms and expectations about professional accountability and responsibility across the system for students' success. Administrators at all levels coordinate resources, guidelines, directives, and other aspects of system operation that affect teachers' professional development.

Administrative support that affects teachers' learning includes, but extends beyond, customary management responsibilities—fiscal accounting, facilities maintenance, and other aspects of "keeping the trains running" efficiently—to include knowledge of teaching and learning, and of the specific efforts teachers are pursuing.

Principals arguably are the most important players affecting the character and consequence of teachers' school-site professional communities. Principals are culture-makers, intentionally or not, and a supportive workplace culture is the bottom-line requirement for a vital learning community. A most important job for principals involves establishing the normative, structural, and practical conditions a teacher learning community needs to thrive. Administrators who see community-building as part of their leadership will give teachers opportunities to collaborate, foster joint work and common language, and provide professional development resources that reinforce teachers' professional growth.

Principals' knowledge and expertise affect teachers' efforts to turn their new knowledge into effective classroom practices. The phrase may be tired, but nonetheless it is true: Effective principals are instructional leaders. Vibrant teacher communities call for principals well versed in content and instruction to provide effective supervision and coaching to their teachers. A New York City district administrator put it this way: "The best professional development happens at the building level every day . . . school leaders being the most important staff developers of all." Principals who understand the arc of classroom work can provide valuable feedback to teachers and assist them in using data in ways that enhance student learning. Useful teacher comment and assistance with classroom reform efforts assume that principals know what they are seeing in a classroom: What does a classroom look like when solid first steps are being taken? When reform is derailed or carried out at a superficial level only? Too few principals possess enough knowledge of academic content and pedagogy to play this role effectively. Many share the worries expressed by a middle school principal: "I'm always asking teachers to do with children what I'm not sure that I can do with them."

Effective process skills are critical to nurturing teacher learning communities because conflict and anxiety are an inevitable by-product of faculty pluralism and diversity—especially as a teacher learning community forms. As chapter 3 elaborates, principals' ability to manage conflict significantly determines whether that community is able to see differences as opportunities for learning and exploration rather than as hurtful, divisive discord that rouses the organization's immune system. Managing conflict productively can, as Roland Barth (2001, p. 73) puts it, send principals' learning curves "off the charts" (see also Achinstein, 2002, for details on how conflict, when managed as a learning resource, contributes to professional community).

Strong learning communities develop when principals learn to relinquish a measure of control and help others participate in building leadership throughout the school. Principals unable to share control with teachers' communities, who seed a climate of suspicion and distrust, or who simply do not value them, quickly squelch teacher learning communities and drive teachers back behind their classroom doors. For example, despite progress at a Students at the Center middle school to build an atmosphere of support, the principal's reluctance to engage race issues within the school's faculty undermined spread and sustainability of improvement efforts within the school. Similarly, principals who joined BASRC Leadership Schools in midcourse of the reform and held norms of practice that differed from those faculties that had developed as part of their inquiry-based reform undercut the foundation of teachers' professional community (McLaughlin & Mitra, 2003). In one elementary school, for example, a teacher commented that his faculty "that was very used to questioning things" just shut down their inquiry-based deliberations when their new principal took a "very by-the-rules approach" and "said this is the way we are going to do it," rather than embracing the open discussions about practice that teachers had grown to value. Teachers in another BASRC elementary school also pointed to their new principal's insistence on being in charge as the main reason their community's inquiry process faltered. One said, "Right after we reached consensus on how we would carry out the Cycle of Inquiry this year, she vetoed it . . . [that shook] our level of trust and belief that we could continue [inquiry]."

Principals manage their school's professional development resources and so hold the key to teachers' site-based ongoing learning. This responsibility is a crucial one from teachers' perspective. For this reason, the National Association of Secondary School Principals (NASSP, 2004, p. 3) put forward "Continuous Professional Development" as one of "Seven Cornerstone Strategies to Improve Student Performance." More specifically, the NASSP recommends that principals support professional learning communities that align school-based professional development resources with individual teachers' "Personal Learning Plans" and with what students need to know and accomplish by the time they graduate.

District administrators' knowledge about reforms under way in the system and the requirements of teacher learning communities affect both principals' and teachers' ability to act on what they've learned and to sustain a school-based learning community. Yet, as a leader of the Philadelphia SATC project remarked to us: "The higher up you go [in the district hierarchy], the less time they [administrators] have, and the greater their unwillingness to really get immersed and to understand what it is you're trying to do. And so it's difficult to get people to make decisions that are supportive of what you need done when they don't really understand the work."

District administrators oversee the system arrangements that can further or frustrate teachers' growth and productive change, as well as principals' efforts to nurture school-based learning communities. Knowledge of the reform work—the academic goals, pedagogical strategies, and implementation issues—is vital as decisions are made about district priorities, the allocation of professional development and other resources, curricula, and assessment choices—decisions that impact on resources and priorities for teachers' learning and classroom practices. Many a school reform effort has foundered when district "in-service" mandates conflicted with a faculty's learning needs or when compliance and reporting demands undermined a school's inquiry strategy. Similarly, district administrators' understanding of the development and contribution of teacher learning communities provides strategic direction for district conceptions of professional development strategies and learning resources for teachers. Chapter 7 elaborates on the vital importance of political and normative leadership, especially the superintendent's, to allocating and protecting the resources necessary to effective site-based learning communities. Further, district leaders enable teacher learning communities by modeling the norms of inquiry and openness essential to a district culture where teacher learning communities thrive. Knowledge about teachers' reform work and the character of learning communities provides the foundation for such leadership.

TEACHERS' ORGANIZATIONS

I don't think it's anything new. It's not rocket science. If you want teachers involved in professional development, you have to get their leaders involved; you have to have their support.
—SATC middle school principal

Teachers' organizations are often missing from accounts of teachers' learning and professional improvement, be they reports on research or reform strategies. For example, Michael Fullan's (2001) comprehensive examination of educational change and relevant actors makes no mention of unions. This omission is a curious and important one. In many districts, teachers' unions are major players in establishing the workplace conditions, supports, and norms that define what, where, and how teachers learn and the expectations to which they are held. Union stance on a district reform agenda and the professional development that goes along with it matters enormously, for better or worse.

Conventional wisdom in the education reform community sees unions as a negative force to be neutralized. For evidence, reformers point to unions' traditional focus on compensation and working conditions as significant roadblocks. Indeed, unions in major cities around the country have frustrated reform efforts when "work to rule" provisions made time for teachers' professional development scarce and contract provisions tied the hands of reformers aiming to develop new standards and measures for classroom effectiveness. For example, the Boston Teacher Union's 6-month job action threatened to cripple the district's

Collaborative, Coaching and Learning (CCL) professional development strategy when work to rule precluded teacher participation in demonstration lessons. Unpleasant experiences with unions lead many reformers to seek only provisional support from teachers' organizations in the form of waivers or exclusions from collective bargaining agreements, where unions are brought into the reform agenda at all.

Yet, while unions can offer some of the most powerful resistance to reform, teachers' organizations also can be essential allies, leaders, or resources for reform. Moreover, it is questionable whether an ambitious learning agenda for teachers can be accomplished without explicit and active union involvement. For instance, the Learning First Alliance's (Togneri & Anderson, 2003) examination of five reforming urban districts describes the importance of district–union partnerships to advance a coherent and ambitious reform agenda.[1] Minneapolis provides a compelling example of union partnership with the district to reform instruction. The union's contract with the district included six standards of effective instruction that featured expectations for teachers' professional growth.[2] Union leaders in Minneapolis stressed teachers' professionalism and worked to remedy unacceptable levels of student performance. Union leaders collaborated with district officials and the school board to develop what the Learning First Alliance's report deemed the "most sophisticated" accountability system found among the five case study districts, using measures of teachers' performance in the classroom. The report concluded that the Minneapolis teachers' union provided a potent force for change in the district. Fulfilling these ambitious expectations for teachers' learning and learning communities required union support and leadership.

San Diego City Schools' reform experience illustrates how the absence of union support for district plans can fuel underlying adversarial relationships between teachers and administrators. Union president Mark Knapp, angered that he had not had a more central role in developing the district's "Blueprint for Change," mobilized teachers' resistance to the district's initiative. Knapp's November 1999 newsletter to teachers described the "emotional abuse [members] suffer daily at the hands of an unthinking, uncaring district." Knapp charged that the district was looking in the wrong direction when it focused on teachers' professional preparation and development as a target for reform. "We aren't stupid," he wrote. "What amazes me most about [San Diego's] fix the broken educator and you will fix the child scapegoat approach is that it is misguided and ignores problems like poverty, attendance, health care, second language learners, etc." (Knapp, 1999, online).

Union leadership in other cities played an essential role in effectively voicing teachers' concerns about reform and brokering agreements. In Providence, for example, teachers expressed worries about unannounced "walkthroughs" by district administrators, which they saw as evaluative and potentially punitive. Union leaders brought those issues to the district, and together they developed a plan for a union representative to accompany district administrators on walkthroughs. These assurances of fairness were discontinued after teachers became comfortable with the expressed coaching and feedback purposes of the visits. In Kent County, Maryland, union leaders and district officials effectively responded to teachers' complaints about centralized, mandated professional development. They formed a professional development council that included teachers, principals, and district staff to guide professional development. Over time, the central office turned over the planning and implementation of professional development entirely to teachers (Togneri & Anderson, 2003, p. 37).

Teachers' organizations around the country have provided critical and unique resources for learning. The Washington Education Association stepped in to address a shortfall in professional development resources created by state budget woes. The union established regional professional learning agencies for teachers (Bascia, 2003). The American Federation of Teachers has focused learning resources to assist in redesigning low-performing schools (American Federation of Teachers, 1999). In New York City, for instance, United Federation of Teachers (UFT) staff worked with district administrators and schools to tailor professional learning programs, especially in underperforming schools. The UFT developed a "resource curriculum" that supports teachers' work in content areas, for instance.

Teacher organizations have championed fundamental reform in labor relations, professional responsibilities, and learning opportunities. Union leaders from 21 urban districts joined together in the mid-1990s to form the Teacher Union Reform Network (TURN). Its primary goal was to "create a new union model" that rests on a "pervasive sense of mutual obligation" and involved a shift from an adversarial to a cooperative model of labor relations (Teacher Union Reform Network, no date). In that spirit of "new unionism," TURN member organizations developed peer review strategies where teachers and unions assumed responsibility for colleagues' performance. New York's United Federation of Teachers operates a peer assistance program to help tenured teachers improve their instructional expertise, and counsels them out of the profession if they cannot improve. Unions in Toledo, Rochester, Seattle, Columbus, and approximately 15 other urban districts operate similar programs. Researchers report that peer review brings higher standards to teaching and links good teaching with professional development. For example, Koppich and Kerchner (1999, p. 323) conclude that "Peer review . . . taps a broader segment of a teacher's professional portfolio through prolonged and extensive engagement with and observation by professional colleagues and an emphasis on enhancing professional practice." Similarly, anecdotal evidence holds that peer review systems are tougher than administrator-driven teacher evaluation strategies.

Unions have been critical resources, too, in mobilizing support for public education generally. Hence, they have played an important role in getting the political and financial support that underwrite teachers' learning. The National Education Association supports communication resources for state and local teachers' organizations to mount public awareness campaigns for education. When budgets have been tight, for instance, the Washington Education Association has launched an effective campaign to gather political support for the state's schools and teachers. The Minneapolis union informed the school board of the opportunities and resources its members would need to tackle the district's ambitious reform agenda. Even in the tumultuous New York City education context, the UFT has been a major force protecting resources for teachers' professional development.

Teachers' organizations are hardly backstage, transitory players in teachers' learning and professional community. Contention between unions and administrators undermine teachers' willingness and ability to engage professional growth opportunities. On the other hand, collaboration and partnership between districts and their unions can boost teachers' learning agenda and professional growth in critical ways. Teachers' organizations can furnish human and financial resources, infrastructure, and political support for learning and professional development across a teacher's career—resources that otherwise might be unavailable.

PROFESSIONAL DEVELOPERS

I am sure we wouldn't be this far without the ongoing involvement of [our support provider]. She knew our school, our kids, and understood what we were trying to accomplish. She was able to hold up a mirror for us to reflect on our practice, and was just so incredibly helpful in bringing in "just in time" resources to support our work.

—BASRC high school teacher

Few schools can stimulate and assist teachers' learning and professional communities without access to outside knowledge resources—that is, access to individuals who can coach on curriculum, advise about inquiry practices, and be a critical friend to teacher learning communities. Chapters 3 and 4 detail the many critical roles professional developers play in nurturing and sustaining teacher learning communities in schools. Schools that lack continuing, dependable access to these resources risk either falling victim to the "competency trap," where faculty become self-satisfied and have no motivation to do things differently, or become discouraged and disaffected because they aren't getting help and encouragement (Levitt & March, 1988).

Professional developers or support providers encompass a range of roles in a widely varied set of organizations, including (but not limited to) nonprofit and for-profit professional development organizations, university-based research and development projects, and national research groups and education labs. Some of these groups specialize in a specific content area, while others focus on curriculum, instruction, assessment, or broader school structure and climate issues. Even within a single professional development organization, professional developers may come from both teaching and non-teaching backgrounds, and bring different kinds of expertise to their work. Professional developers provide ideas, hands-on assistance, and moral support for teachers' learning. They furnish the "curriculum" of teachers' learning communities. In many schools, they play an integral role in guiding and sustaining the reform work because they provide a bridge between professional worlds inside and outside the school.

Their job is an essential and challenging one. The preceding chapters underscore the fundamental contribution professional developers make to teachers' and so to students' learning and to the quality of school-based learning communities. BASRC's experience shows how important the quality and quantity of these learning resources are to teachers' progress and continuing development. BASRC leadership schools struggled to find and employ support providers who would be relevant to their reform efforts, but there were not enough high-quality support providers in the Bay Area to accommodate the needs of nearly a hundred

Leadership Schools. Evaluators found that the school's success in engaging the appropriate support provider did boost results for a Leadership School's reform effort (Center for Research on the Context of Teaching, 2002). Without a productive relationship with a support provider, school reform efforts and teachers' learning stalled, especially in schools challenged by poverty and the pressing needs of an ethnically and culturally diverse student body.

BASRC's Phase 2 reform featured coaching as a strategy to expand and intensify the support provider role. School coach positions were funded to work closely with "focal school" faculty on a reform agenda. This strategy highlighted the importance of coach knowledge, but did not support it. Coaches in BASRC Phase 2 also were asked to help teachers with literacy efforts, but many were not prepared to do that. District administrators observed: "To be a coach takes knowledge of instruction that not all of the [district] coaches currently have." Beyond instructional expertise, coaches were called on to help teachers move ahead with the Cycle of Inquiry, BASRC's hallmark. They had little capacity to provide this support. Said one on expectations that coaches would assist with schools with the Cycle of Inquiry: "I can't lead [inquiry] because I can't do it myself" (Coggins, 2005). A coach skilled in Cycle of Inquiry described a session she led for coaches: "I put out some of the basic vocabulary words [associated with inquiry]—normal curve, criterion reference, diagnostic assessment. Most coaches sat there in stunned silence when I ask them to match term to definition." One teacher said, "I couldn't do one." BASRC coaches' efforts to assist classroom change fell short of expectations, largely because they lacked the skills and knowledge needed to assist teachers' change efforts.

STAKEHOLDERS: PARENTS AND COMMUNITY MEMBERS

Nowhere is the two-way street of learning more in disrepair and in need of social reconstruction than that concerning the relationship among parents, communities and their schools.
                                        —(Fullan, 2001, p. 198)

Stakeholders relevant to teachers' learning and community include everyone from parents to members of the school board, the business community, and the civic elite. An engaged public plays an indispensable role in school reform and support for public education. *It Takes a City*, advises the title of the book on urban school reform by Paul Hill, Christine Campbell, and James Harvey (2000). Teachers' motivation and ability to learn, and to implement that learning in the classroom, depend on the support of the larger community. Schools are not institutional islands. Parent and community attitudes, expectations, and knowledge affect teachers' classroom efforts and schools' reform goals in many fundamental ways. Some of these connections are substantive—for example, parents are an underutilized way to reinforce teachers' efforts in the home. Parents who understand classroom activities and goals can extend teachers' opportunity to teach into homes and neighborhoods. Compelling, consistent evidence shows how parent and teacher learning can be mutually reinforcing and lead to improved student achievement (see, for example, Henderson & Mapp, 2002). Similarly, when teachers and parents have respectful, trusting relationships, schools can more effectively create and sustain connections that strengthen both student and teacher learning. Education then becomes a collaborative endeavor.

The moral, financial, and political support given by these stakeholders have many effects. The "math wars" dampened teachers' enthusiasm and ability to use the new mathematics practices they were learning, for example, and led many teachers to abandon the effort (and in some cases the profession) in the face of parental objections. At the community level, civic support for specific reform efforts and for the public schools plays a crucial part in teachers' sense of being valued for their efforts. In one locale, where community leaders and the media engaged in weekly criticisms of the schools, teachers told us that they were embarrassed to admit in social gatherings that they were teachers. These teachers, not surprisingly, had little motivation to consider how they might improve their classroom practices. Likewise, ignorance about what schools are trying to accomplish and the resources they need sometimes lead civic leaders to make choices that undermine the stability of teachers' instructional agenda and the resources associated with it (Stone, Henig, Jones, & Pierannunzi, 2001).

The informed and articulated support of the larger community—financial, emotional, and logistical—motivates teachers to invest in learning and creates support for teacher professional development. According to research, trustees on school boards viewed as most successful in terms of their leadership of a strong, coherent instructional program also were more knowledgeable about district programs and practices, had clear goals for instruction, and held firm beliefs about the kinds of practices they wanted to see in their schools (LaRocque & Coleman, cited in Fullan, 2001, p. 82).

Support for public education and teachers' professional growth also demands the backing of the civic elite—that is, the opinion-setters whose views influence funding and political favor. Few dispute how important it is that community members are informed about teachers' efforts and support them. Their views affect not only elected officials (such as school boards) but also the private and nonprofit sector, valuable allies for public education. Clarence Stone and colleagues (2001) and Paul Hill and colleagues (2000), observers of urban education reform efforts, stress the importance of building coalitions around urban school reform. Similarly, Robert Sexton (2004) elaborates how the Pritchard Committee for Academic Excellence created and sustained a campaign to educate the public about the challenges facing Kentucky's public schools. The committee galvanized support from mainstream civic organizations and the general public to pass and fund the complex and far-reaching 1990 Kentucky Education Reform Act; more than a decade later, backing from the public continues to focus state politicians and civic leaders on school reform. Stone, Hill, and Sexton emphasize that stakeholders include not only professional educators and parents, but politicians, nonprofits, employers, seniors, and others. Broad-based coalitions impart civic support that brings stability, encouragement, and, often, resources to teachers' learning and practice. For example, Henderson and Mapp (2002) describe how organized community efforts to improve low-performing schools in poor urban communities and the rural South appear to be succeeding.

However, effective, broad-based coalitions are so difficult to build and sustain that few good examples exist. The negative effects when broad civic support is missing are clearer. For instance, community leaders in San Antonio and Charlotte ignored board elections, so a disaffected group of teachers successfully encouraged voters to replace reformers on the board; in the process, they undermined the efforts of teachers who supported the reforms (Hill et al., 2000). District leaders in San Diego dedicated significant resources to implementing their blueprint for change. However, they failed to communicate their plans to the broader community or even to parents. Their neglect came close to overturning the reform, as one part of the community threatened to secede from the district. A close school board race came within one seat of electing a board that almost certainly would have removed the superintendent and changed the reform's course. Similarly, Liane Brouillette (1996) documents how conflicting ideas within the community about reform goals and strategies capsized a district's restructuring effort. She maintains that open discussion and consensus-building efforts are indispensable to successful school reform.

Ignorance about local needs, teachers' professional goals, and plans for more effective classroom practices poses a fundamental barrier to getting parents and the community behind teachers' efforts. In many instances, these stakeholders simply have no information about what teachers are up to. But beyond that, ideas about "the way things used to be," outmoded mental models of school, often thwart teachers' initiatives and learning goals. Parents and community members need opportunities to move beyond old notions of education, based on how they remember they were educated, and understand basic tenets and challenges of new practice.

In sum, teachers' ability to learn and to act on that learning, and the sustained vitality of their learning communities, depend on the attitudes and actions of others in the broader context. The extent to which administrators, parents, community leaders, and others further or frustrate teachers' learning communities and improvement efforts depends to a significant extent on what they know and understand about teachers' work. From this perspective, in order for teachers' learning to be effective, everyone in the local context must be a learner. What resources and opportunities support a local learning agenda?

6

Everyone a Learner: Challenges and Promising Practices

Administrators, professional developers, and community stakeholders play vital roles in teachers' professional lives and communities. What learning opportunities and resources focus on these key actors? A scan of local education landscapes yields a fairly dismal picture: When learning opportunities associated with education reform efforts are planned, administrators typically are ignored; professional development organizations, district support providers, and community members generally are completely overlooked. The first matter of business in supporting teachers' learning and professionalism, therefore, is to move these actors into local reform plans. Next we consider the challenges of informing these actors about teachers' work. Finally, we describe practices that have succeeded.

SYSTEM ADMINISTRATORS

As reform plans are drawn up, district administrators' professional development is decidedly on a back burner. Learning opportunities for central office staff are slim. Where they occur, they usually focus on management issues, not instructional issues or teaching and learning goals. Ironically, the people who ultimately have the greatest responsibility for charting a clear course for teaching and learning in a school system in fact have the fewest opportunities for professional growth. Reformers ignore the learning needs of the central office, which is responsible for articulating and supporting the district's goals for teachers and students. Tellingly, reports of district "capacity," or accounts of district fiscal resources, instructional supports, and resources for teachers' professional development, almost never include the knowledge and instructional expertise of central office administrators.

Principals do not fare much better. "It's a vacuum for principals," complained an urban school leader about district professional development resources. Despite an apparent appetite for collegial exchange, district or initiative-based learning communities for principals are rarely considered when issues concerning district capability to undertake and sustain school reform are addressed. A principal involved in the Philadelphia SATC initiative commented on how seldom reform efforts include administrators:

> I've been involved in dozens of programs, and this is the first grant that structured a program for administrators. It seems like common sense, but evidently it's not so common! It's one thing for me to push my teachers into professional development. It is quite another for me to sit down for a series of professional development activities . . . and come back to the school not just preaching but really modeling the kind of behavior I expect and want from teachers. Many times teachers have said to me, "I was at a class last night." And I can say, "So was I."

Administrators are the first to acknowledge that it is tough to engage them in productive learning opportunities—administrative demands, discipline problems, nonstop parent requests, meetings and meetings, district accountability requirements, and a raft of other, often unpredictable pressures take up their time, energy, and attention. Nonetheless, the professional isolation they experience is wearisome. An elementary school principal reflected:

> It's difficult when you are a principal. When you are a teacher, you have a cadre of people to go to. You have a support group in your building. You can go to the reading specialist, and the principal, the library. You can go to a cadre of people for help. When you're the principal . . . where can you go for help?

When offered, however, the quality of such learning opportunities often disappoints. Principals, like teachers, say that their available professional development menu more often than not is of marginal value. While the principals' roles and responsibilities have changed, professional development has not changed to meet them. The traditional higher education principal preparation programs— "Ed Admin 101"— are generally disconnected from the daily realities of schools, and seldom anchored in hands-on, school-based leadership experience. On-the-job support for administrators' learning is weak. It hardly ever focuses on instructional issues but generally features management issues identified by the district or information about the latest regulatory or compliance issues.

Even where administrators' learning needs have been considered, opportunities to address them have been difficult to establish for structural and substantive reasons. Administrators say efforts are often too general to be relevant, inconvenient, or just of poor quality. The Bay Area School Reform Collaborative, for example, tried to create a regional principals' network—an occasion for principals from reforming schools to convene around their reform efforts. The effort was rocky from the outset. High school principals felt that their colleagues at elementary schools struggled with problems significantly different in kind and degree. Many participants thought the content was uneven in quality or relevance to their setting. And almost all participants said that the time commitment—which included significant Bay Area travel time—was just too much (Center for Research on the Context of Teaching, 2002).

While learning occasions for district administrators are few and far between,[1] opportunities for principals' professional development are slowly improving. Reformers and policymakers have become more aware of the need to provide administrators with high-quality, instruction-focused learning opportunities, and the need to provide these learning resources in a convenient, relevant format. As a result, state-run leadership academies have sprung up, some reforms have started to include professional development for administrators alongside supports for teachers, and organizations now exist that focus solely on the learning needs of administrators.

In Philadelphia, administrator institutes associated with the Students at the Center initiative provide a good example of productive learning resources for administrators. The institute comprised elementary-middle-high schools that made up student feeder patterns. The institutes' curriculum centered on the student-focused practices that defined the reform effort. Participating principals unanimously praised the administrator institutes because they provided occasion for peer interaction and because the agenda was focused on their learning, not on administrative issues. They especially lauded the institute's attention to strengthening their process skills as particularly valuable to their teacher community-building efforts. One Philadelphia principal told us:

> The [institute courses] have changed me as an administrator tremendously. I am less didactic. I am more open. I don't feel threatened [when people disagree] and try to identify problems in a nonthreatening way and include more people in the solution—to build community in my school. I knew I needed this but didn't know where to go for help.

The former New York City District 3 offers another rich example of how district-organized efforts can give principals the knowledge they need to support teachers' learning and community in their schools. The district established monthly, full-day leadership conferences intended to inform principals about the district's priorities and instructional initiatives and, in the words of a district administrator, "get them information they can bring to their teachers, [to help] teachers implement practice . . . based on the district's beliefs" (Center for the Study of Teaching and Policy, no date). Leadership conferences focused heavily on providing principals the skills and knowledge they would need to be instructional leaders. The conferences illustrated the kind of teaching and learning district leaders wanted to see in their schools—problem-based, interactive, and learner-focused. For example, one day's activities touched on the district's literacy and math initiative and included:

- A District 2 principal modeling a "literature response circle"
- A presentation by the deputy superintendent on connections among literacy, teaching, and assessment
- A teacher-led examination of the standards for a response-to-reading to be included in a student's portfolio
- Reflections on the nature of "mathematical communication" and a study of selected pages from the National Council of Teachers of Mathematics's *Principles and Standards for School Mathematics*
- Small-group discussions of classroom environments that support mathematics communication.

District 3 also brought resources into underperforming schools to help principals make necessary changes in instruction. To support school leadership, the principals of priority schools developed mentoring relationships with individual district leaders—deputy and assistant superintendents, directors of curriculum. The mentors spent substantial time in their assigned schools, building trust, trying to understand the school, and providing technical assistance. Additionally, principals of high-priority schools had "think tank" meetings—monthly gatherings with the superintendent in a smaller group than the regular monthly principal conferences. The deputy superintendent described his role in this process as that of a teacher: "I did a guided reading lesson on the floor with kids. . . . The unstated goal is for me to model [for principals] that I want them on the floor with children and teachers."

These examples from Philadelphia and New York are positive and instructive, but relatively modest in scale. In what could be the nation's most intensive and expensive professional development for principals, the San Diego City Schools has initiated concentrated learning opportunities for *all* of the district's principals. Professional development for principals forms the core of San Diego's ambitious, systemwide reform effort; it comprises the primary strategy for creating instructional coherence across the system. Every principal of the district's 180 schools was required to participate in intensive, ongoing professional development both on and off their school campus, beginning in August 1998 when Anthony Alvarado, San Diego's newly appointed chancellor of instruction, rolled out the district reform plan. Principals' knowledge, leadership skills, and understanding of the district's reform plans were put front and center because principals would be held accountable for the instructional quality in their schools and student outcomes.

To fulfill this role, the district invested in multiple reinforcing approaches to build principals' ability to recognize high-quality instruction and lead it. Principals were cast in a turnkey role—"carriers" of instructional knowledge to their campuses, with responsibility for bringing what they had learned in various district-sponsored professional development sessions to their teachers. The district was restructured with an eye to principals' ongoing learning and reflection. Seven learning communities were created that brought principals together monthly under the leadership of a newly created district-level position, Instructional Leader (IL). Alvarado hand-picked the ILs, all former principals, as proven, outstanding educational leaders; their work with principals is ongoing. In their learning communities, ILs offer principals additional coaching and instruction, and principals discuss the array of materials assigned by their IL. In addition, ILs focus on school leadership and fostering the qualities it requires. Principals participate in other monthly meetings as well: for grade levels; reading groups; and various peer activities, such as cohort meetings, that involve actively critiquing one another's practices.

The ILs follow up with frequent visits to their principals' schools and use "walkthroughs" or "learning walks" to coach principals on what to look for in teachers' instruction and classroom environment. They also coach principals on providing professional development to their teachers; videotapes of these principal-led sessions are critiqued by the principals' learning community as a way to construct the capacity of members through analysis of their own and others' leadership. ILs also assess how principals are incorporating what they are learning about deepening instructional practice into their work with teachers; they also assess what the principal and staff should concentrate on next. ILs routinely meet with principals to discuss instruction and student work in individual classrooms; they ask about how the school leader has responded to problems evident in student outcomes or during walkthroughs. Visits from district staff provide additional feedback on the principals' instructional leadership. And starting in the 4th year of the reform, the ILs assigned a staff developer to each school, to coach the principal and teachers on instructional strategies.

Principals also attend monthly conferences with their peers; its aim is to bring coherence across districts. At first, the conferences included principals only. By the 5th year, the principals' conferences became learning conferences and included more site-based individuals—vice principals, administrative interns, content administrators, and occasionally peer coaches. While this expansion doubles, trebles, and even quadruples attendance and hampers small-group conversations, "the trade-offs have been huge," according to one IL, who added, "the VPs are much more prepared, and the interns are also." Principals note that their own interactions during these conferences are evolving. For instance, they have begun to explore the mechanisms behind *why* the techniques they are learning are successful; they have also started to brainstorm implementation strategies for their schools. They say that this active questioning and group discovery process is a key element in turning ideas into knowledge and knowledge into practice.

While San Diego principals worry about the new, additional responsibilities on their plates, they are also buoyed by this now-formalized instructional leadership role. As one told us: "I've never been more challenged or more enthusiastic in 30 years! It's so exciting because it's research-based. Some of the training has really enlivened me to be a better administrator and a better instructional leader." Teachers in this principal's school say that her enthusiasm has been contagious, and that the principal has made support for their professional development available on-site.

Another longtime principal reflected on the principals' professional development this way: "It's been very, very complete. . . . The in-service training that we had before [Alan Bersin and Anthony Alvarado instituted the 1998 blueprint reform] was isolated pieces that we didn't connect later. Different people had different approaches to it. But this was streamlined. We were all talking the same language, and I learned a body of research with which I later was able to raise student achievement."

Survey data reinforce the principals' value for their professional learning, and their judgment that their roles have changed as a result. In a May 2004 survey of San Diego principals, the majority report that they find the array of professional development resources "valuable" or "extremely valuable," and approximately 80% report that the time they spend on instructional leadership in their schools has "increased greatly" since the reform began. Teachers say that this focus on principals as key change agents in schools directly affects their practice. For example, teachers from several schools mentioned that the principals' classroom observations have increased in frequency and depth, that feedback about practice is more immediate and specific, and that instructional coherence in the school is growing as a consequence.

PROFESSIONAL DEVELOPERS

School reform depends on the people involved in it, and the quality of professional developers is arguably the most important ingredient for its success, whether in a school or district. An uneven quality of professional developers yields uneven results. If the learning coordinators' skills are out of sync with reform priorities or if they lack necessary expertise, they compromise a teacher's learning. Yet as vital as this external resource is to teachers' learning, along with their ability to implement that learning effectively, they often operate as "independent agents," struggling on their own to acquire the skills and knowledge they need to be effective (see, e.g., Richard, 2003). Unfortunately, few reformers or policymakers acknowledge that professional developers—be they independent consultants or district employees—also need ongoing learning opportunities. Hence, it is no surprise that few exist for them. As one Bay Area support provider explained, "It's a really difficult job . . . there isn't enough support for support providers! We're doing our best, but we don't necessarily have the training that we wish we did. . . . I don't think the structures we have in place right now at all support providers' [professional development needs]." Yet the consequences of inadequate learning resources for professional developers are significant at both individual and system levels. When their expertise erodes, professionals diminish as a resource for teachers' learning and learning communities. At the system level, unless support providers can harmonize their experiences and expertise, they may fragment reform efforts and send conflicting messages to teachers and principals.

Professional developers' learning agenda parallels that of teachers. Obviously, professional developers must keep abreast of new ideas and theories within their areas of expertise. Ironically, many professional developers, support providers, learning coordinators, and teacher educators cannot support teachers in mastering the more complex forms of teaching because they have not mastered them themselves. Professional developers must themselves learn and change their practice to support the ambitious and challenging nature of contemporary reforms. Their work with teachers many times reflects a paradigm of teaching based in demonstration, practice, and facts rather than the beliefs and habits of practice that underlie reformers' agenda (Coggins, 2005). The learning agenda for professional developers calls for rethinking ideas about learning and classroom roles. Further, many professional developers need a comprehensive repertoire because they find themselves working with a wide variety of teachers in very different forums. One professional developer may be facilitating an off-site course for high school teachers while concurrently doing classroom consulting work at the elementary level. Responding to the needs of individual teachers and diverse school settings requires a content and pedagogical foundation that is both broad and deep within a professional developer's area or areas of specialty. Professional developers also must know how to work effectively with diverse learners—that is, teachers at different points in their own development, knowledge, and skill.

Professional developers generally have been prepared to work with individual teachers but not with learning communities (Stein, Smith, & Silver, 1999). They confront the same difficulties teachers do when they strive to change their classroom from traditional "sage on the stage" format to create a learning community of students. Work with a community of practice calls for a different teaching frame and different conceptions of knowledge and learning. Professional developers lacking the knowledge and skill to work effectively with learning communities or to assist both the community and individuals in learning new ways of working can undermine reform goals. Work with communities of teachers brings new process goals to professional developers' purview—teachers want assistance with such areas as conflict resolution skills, community-building, evidence-based discussion, and leadership development. And professional developers need to learn how to work collaboratively with teachers, rather than bringing in a set curriculum and agenda—the typical workshop format—and they need to give teachers an active role in constructing knowledge. To this point, professional developers associated with the Philadelphia's Students at the Center project claim that if professional development is not based on a collegial relationship with teachers, they will be unable to form productive working relationships. The professional developers stress the importance of "careful listening skills" to help teachers unpack issues, reflect, and help the developers consider what the teacher learner brings to the effort in terms of classroom experiences. Similarly, based on their observation of professional developers working to bring a new mathematics curriculum into schools, Mary Kay Stein, Margaret Smith, and Edward Silver (1999, p. 266) conclude that professional developers "must not only develop teachers as individuals, but also grow self-sustaining learning communities and put into place instructional programs that reach across the grades."

The nature of the job itself, as well as the funding and reform environment, keep professional developers from getting the learning resources they need. Some support providers, such as members of the National Writing Project or the Coalition of Essential Schools, find learning resources within their own organization—but they are the exception. Most professional development organizations are too small and overextended to support their members' learning needs—and so limit their effectiveness.

However, even when support providers find occasions to address their learning needs, the structure of their work frustrates their ability to participate. In particular, they often don't have time for profitable discussion among themselves. Bay Area support providers associated with BASRC Leadership Schools found, for instance, that their already time-pressured job, coupled with the logistics of coordinating appointments with colleagues in different schools, severely limited meaningful time together. As one support provider explained, it's hard to justify spending time talking with other support providers when "we're not funded to do that . . . we're funded to be out in the schools doing the work we're supposed to do." Support providers often cannot find the time to model the processes of inquiry and reflection that they want their schools to adopt.

And because many support providers must be entrepreneurs in business for themselves, anxiety about competition and lost business dampens their interest in a learning community of their own. One explained:

> I think all support providers are in a precarious position about
> bringing in enough money to support their work. And so if I go
> into a support provider meeting, and I say, "Hey, here's what's
> working well at this school and here's what isn't working well,"
> you can bet that some support provider will be on the phone to my
> school saying, "Hey, I can fill this need." That's the big reason why
> nobody's talking.

What kinds of opportunities have overcome these structural and resource hurdles? Stein et al. (1999) note that little, if any, research examines effective learning supports for professional developers. Not surprisingly, given what we know about how adults learn, professional developers' best learning opportunities exist in learning communities of their peers. The Philadelphia Students at the Center (SATC) project partnered professional developers and teacher educators from three distinctly different organizations, PhilWP (the district's writing project), the Franklin Institute (a science museum), and Beaver College's teacher education department. These organizations and individuals had not worked together before launching the SATC project. Every one of them cited their collaboration as the most stimulating and transforming professional learning of their careers. They became a learning community as they co-designed curriculum, action plans, and meetings; as they struggled to understand one another's assumptions about teaching and learning; and as they discussed the finer points of their different content bases— science, writing and teacher education. According to one of them, "Our partner meetings were intense, sustained, and unique to the Philadelphia SATC. That was the environment where we developed trust and respect, a laboratory where we could bring our practices and share them, try to make sense of them, work together as partners." They modeled practice for one another, and so enabled colleagues to see how their similar theories of teaching and learning manifested in different contents. Franklin Institute and PhilWP, for example, collaborated in providing a summer institute on writing in science classes for SATC teachers and parents. To plan and carry out the institute, science educators from the Franklin Institute required instruction from PhilWP staff in the principles of writing, and similarly, writing teachers had to learn about science. "You have to know enough about something to pose a good writing prompt," said a PhilWP staff member, "and you learn the most when you're in a situation where you don't know the answer." Her colleague from the Franklin Institute echoed the same theme when explaining why the SATC project was a powerful learning community:

> From the beginning, I was called on to do a bunch of things and be in a bunch of situations that required skills I really didn't have. But this project gave us both the requirement and the opportunity to move beyond our comfort level, to find out other things we could do. It was appropriate because we were asking teachers to take risks, so, in a way, it's only fair that we would have to be doing it, too.

Another Franklin Institute science educator commented that the most powerful part of the project for her was "association with like-minded and not like-minded colleagues. The different perspectives kept ideas bouncing. The thing that helped me a lot was sharing. Previously I have always learned in isolation—do it for yourself!" Philadelphia SATC's powerful learning community for professional developers reflected project leaders' beliefs that they needed to be learners, too, and have the support of a community as they proceeded with their new work.

New York's Students at the Center project created an even more ambitious learning community for its consultants. New York SATC, like the Philadelphia project, brought individuals and organizations into partnership for the first time. New York SATC involved nine diverse professional development organizations: the New York City Math Project, the New York City Writing Project, Elementary Teachers' Network—all housed at Lehman College in the Bronx—two reading and writing projects at Teachers College in Manhattan, the Science Workshop Center at City College, the Educational Video Center, the American Social History Project at Teachers College, and Youth Communications, Incorporated. The teacher consultants associated with each organization initiated a community of practice so that they could learn about one another's classroom work. In so doing, they hoped to deepen their own practice and work together as partners in schools. In the 1st year, they began monthly meetings. By the 2nd year, they had scheduled four Saturday workshops to bring together consultants and teachers from all SATC schools. Each workshop, led by a team of consultants, had a specific focus: looking at student work, assessment, writing for publication, and looking at teaching practice.

In a panel discussion at the end of the SATC project, New York consultants were unanimous in praising the effect this learning community had for their practice, their effectiveness in schools, and their professional growth. They also agreed that this community made SATC a coherent project, rather than a loose federation of nine disconnected professional development organizations. As one consultant reflected, "Our group created those sessions for us, it wasn't anyone's work, it wasn't the Math Project's work or the Writing Project's work. It was SATC work. And that was really important because we all had to give up our individual project identities. We all were taking risks by moving outside our own comfort zone."

By the final year, these sessions had fostered close professional bonds and deep trust—and laughter. But it was not always so. Consultants tell of a difficult, tension-filled first year of community-building; their reflections on it provide important developmental signposts. Each consultant brought a strong professional and organizational identity to the project, as well as important differences in how they provided professional development, worked with teachers, or set up schedules in the schools. Said one, "We were very much in our own box with our own established reputations. There was a real fear of letting go of our identity. We were intrigued by the idea of working together but had no idea what it meant to partner with a teacher consultant from another organization." The presentations consultants made about their work during that 1st year elicited their feelings of vulnerability and competitiveness. Later, consultants stressed how much that initial environment felt risky to them because many of the participants were strangers and many of their organizations competed for the same business.

The group developed strategies that enabled them to move beyond these concerns to construct a strong learning community. Participants developed protocols and formal procedures for the meetings that dissolved anxieties about appearing incompetent or uninformed before peers (what one participant aptly dubbed "consultant shame"). The group agreed on norms and behaviors for the meetings; it created protocols they would all use when presenting and critiquing work or readings. The agenda for most of the presentations was similar—presentation, reflection on the presentation, lunch, and business items such as upcoming events and schedules. The result of this codification of community behavior was a significant increase in trust and comfort, in what a consultant called "a very democratic kind of way of responding and working together to ensure that everybody was heard, every voice got raised in those presentations, both the presenters and the listeners." Another consultant elaborated:

As a result of the norms developed for Saturday seminars we became secure enough [to be] able to present work and look at it critically, though supportively. The presentations became so powerful and so important. We all felt we were learning so much from them. Not only about each other's practice, but about each other's school contexts—it was so helpful to be able to talk [about] some of the pedagogical and curricular issues we were confronting at particular schools.

The shared language that developed during the course of the group's discussions was an essential aspect of the participants' learning; so were the understandings the group realized. And, as is always the case, comfort and candor took a while to surface. Consultants believe that many of the issues and frustrations of their 1st year were a result of "just a different language." When consultants got to the point where they understood each other sufficiently to argue, "the learning and the laughter started. We were all so very serious at first," recalled a writing consultant.

Consultants described several positive consequences of the learning community they created. Strong cross-organization work occurred in the schools, planned jointly by participating organizations, so no one discipline or approach dominated. Co-development brought new knowledge and perspective to participating consultants. Consultants from the history project learned video techniques from the Educational Video Center, for instance, while video consultants learned about the American Revolution. Much stronger relationships between consultants led some to teach courses together in schools. These collaborations also led to changes in consultants' professional development organizations, as participants learned from one another and saw more effective ways to work with teachers and schools. The evolution of New York SATC's learning community for teacher consultants has lessons for us, both about the particular contribution it made to individual and organizational capacity, and about strategies for creating an environment where all feel safe and respected—an essential condition for learning.

It is significant that these learning communities were fashioned by SATC partners, educators who placed conceptions of communities of learners at the heart of their work with teachers. It is understandable that they would turn to a learning community as necessary to the success of the SATC project in their settings. But these were foundation-funded special projects. District support for professional developers' learning and skill-building is much more unusual. The experience of San Diego's Instructional Leaders over the course of the reform underscores the significance of learning opportunities for these lead district professional developers, and a cautionary tale about their absence.

San Diego ILs' learning needs were a prominent consideration from the beginning of the reform effort. Since they were responsible for designing and providing professional development for the districts' principals, the ILs needed to have deep knowledge of reform precepts, strategies, and expectations. Alvarado outlined an intense curriculum for them—one designed to provide firsthand experience with the practices he wanted to see in San Diego schools, and to produce a consistent, coherent message as individual ILs worked with their Learning Communities and principals.

The ILs learned to work closely with one another. Through their own professional learning opportunities, they developed what they called "a single voice"—common understandings and judgments about quality instructional practice. For the first two years, ILs received training directly from Alvarado. He turned over this role to Elaine Fink when she came to San Diego to lead the newly created Educational Leadership Development Academy. Alvarado and Fink facilitated structured learning activities for the ILs, including connecting them with learning specialists at the Learning Research and Development Center (LRDC) in Pittsburgh, accomplished instructional leaders from District 2 in New York, and organizational and leadership experts like Michael Fullan and Richard Elmore to help them better understand systems change. Fink also began videotaping ILs as they worked with groups of principals, so they could later review and debrief their own practice with her and other ILs. In addition, she would accompany ILs on school visits, observing and coaching them as they worked with principals. With Fink and Alvarado, training was ongoing, intense, and at times deeply personal. Every IL characterized it as a powerful (if sometimes painful) mechanism for learning and growth in these roles.

By the 6th year of the reform, when Alvarado had retired from the district and Fink's role became more focused on principal development, ILs' professional development became less structured and primarily self-initiated. All the ILs, from the original and subsequent cohorts, saw this switch as problematic, whether it was caused by budget cuts, Alvarado's and Fink's exodus as IL trainers, lack of time, or simple neglect. Typical remarks: "I miss us not being spurred by someone"; "We never go out of the district anymore, out of house, to observe what other people are doing"; "My fear is that we have not continued our own learning."

Professional developers are a fundamental resource for principals' and teachers' professional development, yet policymakers overlook them. This state of affairs is ironic because the developers arguably represent the most important investment in teachers' learning, both through direct work with teachers and by building principals' capabilities as instructional leaders. Professional developers' own learning has to be front and center in reformers' plans.

PARENTS

Traditional parent involvement strategies center on what parents can do to enhance classroom activities in the home—reading to their children, monitoring homework, taking them to libraries and museums. Research demonstrates these strategies' value to students and their teachers. Other popular parent programs focus on better informing parents about school and their children's education. Parents, especially those who were not educated in the United States or who have received little formal schooling, benefit from learning how the school operates, how to become involved, and how to support their children's academic success. Knowledge of the curriculum and pedagogy being used in the classroom is especially important when classroom work departs significantly from how the parents themselves were taught.

Schools' efforts to involve parents can greatly enhance teachers' capacity to use the knowledge they have gained from professional development opportunities and to extend opportunities to learn into the home. However, typical parent involvement strategies are unidirectional; they put the school in charge of parents' learning agenda and operate on an expert-based delivery model of instruction. They focus on what families lack rather than on the beliefs, values, and knowledge that parents can contribute to the school setting. Thus they generally don't affect teachers' own learning. Most promising as resources for teachers' professional growth, and more uncommon, are initiatives that engage parents and teachers together in hands-on learning efforts that model the kinds of practices teachers use in the classroom and involve parents directly in students' projects. These efforts inevitably involve learning by both participants, parents learning about teachers' classroom activities and teachers learning about their students' home contexts and needs.

Parent programs that situate parents' learning agenda squarely in classroom work are less common because of the nature of the resources required and because of the relationship assumed between parent and teacher. Most teachers are interested in parents taking a "support" rather than collaborative role in their classroom practice, citing reasons of professional expertise, status, and, when candid, personal comfort. A challenge for creating powerful relationships between parents and teachers involves how to address parents' learning needs and worries while also allowing teachers and parents to assume new roles with each other. Both the Philadelphia and the Chicago Students at the Center projects successfully met these challenges. Both explicitly defined a substantive partner role for parents—a relationship that benefited teachers, their students, and parents.

By all accounts, the Parent Project was one of Chicago SATC's most successful efforts.[2] Well over 1,000 parents participated in at least one of the six-meeting cycles of the project. Parent Project participants went on to lead groups of students in classrooms and field trips, participate in local school councils, and lobby the city government for improvements in their schools and neighborhoods. Furthermore, as the demand for new Parent Projects grew, experienced parent participants founded and led new Parent Projects at other schools.

The Parent Project empowered parents by integrating them into the core work of the school. For instance, parents at several schools were trained to work with small groups of students in the school garden and on field trips doing scientific tests. Others were involved in the classroom and the school in a more general way—for instance, parents at Jenner School organized an all-day "It Takes a Village to Raise a Child" series of workshops and "raised hell" at city hall until a new school was built, finding ways to support teachers politically. Still others became involved with the local school councils. As one principal said, "These are the same parents who eventually end up on a local school council and our bilingual committee. We don't have to draft anybody anymore."

Chicago's Parent Project believed that for families to support teachers as they put students in a more active learning role, parents needed to understand and experience such teaching practices themselves. The content of each Parent Project varied, to accommodate different schools and different activities. For example, at Waters School, the Parent Project emphasized the schoolwide theme of ecology and the arts. On one day, parents used magnifying glasses in the garden, drew what they observed, wrote metaphors for what they saw, and then hypothesized about why nature created what they had observed in that particular way. At the end of the meeting, a teacher read a Puerto Rican story about a garden to model good read-aloud techniques. The parents' homework was to take a walk with their children, during which they were to ask the children to look at plants and flowers through a magnifying glass and hypothesize about why they looked that way. They then recorded their children's observations in a journal. This way, the children saw their parents writing and doing homework. Parents, teachers, administrators, and classroom aides at Waters all agreed that the Parent Project has been instrumental in helping parents understand a way of teaching that is very different from the way they were taught.

A cornerstone of the Parent Project's success was its emphasis on building community to support the school and its teachers—efforts that contributed to an atmosphere in which teachers and parents shared concerns openly. Teachers appreciated the new relationships with parents and described the many ways parents contributed to their professional growth. For example, a teacher at Waters, one of Chicago's high-poverty elementary schools, told us, "I think it has brought me as a teacher, as a faculty member, into a place that my colleagues don't often get a chance to experience. To see the parents as social people, as whole people, and to understand their children better." A teacher at Jenner, a school that served one of Chicago's most notorious housing projects, echoed this thought:

> I've been able to tap into parents whom I've come to see as responsible for field trips. And I don't just mean field trips like can you come with me because I need somebody to watch these kids. I mean parents who are on board with me philosophically, intellectually . . . they understand me as an art teacher, and they know my goals and understand what I'm about. They know the work I'm doing with their own kids.

Philadelphia's SATC project extended its student-centered pedagogy to parents' learning in similar ways. Parents and teachers attended summer institutes lasting several weeks, where they learned together about new classroom strategies and the student-centered pedagogical stance central to the initiative. After the institute, parents and teachers attended three retreats during the year to reflect on the project's work in their schools. The project also sponsored a Parent Center, where parents from across the district cluster—an elementary, middle, and high school student feeder pattern—could share experiences and ideas. The goal was to establish a partnership between teachers and parents so that they could facilitate better classroom experiences for the children. According to the director of the Philadelphia program, "My main vision is that parents will really learn what good instruction looks like and they'll know the right kinds of questions to ask. That can only lead to kids doing much better." Parents who participated in the SATC institute agreed that what they learned not only helped them make valuable contributions in the school, but also allowed them to be more knowledgeable supports for their children at home. One parent put it this way:

> So with your being here and seeing different ways to approach a subject, and teach that subject, you have something to work with at home. It helps a lot. You're learning what the child is studying in school so that you can go home with that child and work with them. Rather than depending on the child, who oftentimes has not a clue . . . even though they sat in class. And more textbooks are coming home. Which is big. Instead of just the workbook without the textbook to go with it. What good is a workbook to a parent who has not an idea what the workbook is for?

After their involvement in SATC summer institutes, parents became classroom partners to teachers in their schools. This partnership involved them in substantive activities in which they assumed responsible roles—a far cry from the classroom photocopying and lunch money collection tasks typically assigned to teachers' aides. The Philadelphia SATC project director described the learning that continued as parents became involved in classrooms: "They're in classrooms, they're seeing instruction, and for a large number of our parents they were actually in the classroom with their own children as the instruction was taking place. Because of their involvement with the institute, they know about the multiple literacies of their child outside of school and inside the school [and can support them]." She sees how the partnership benefited PSATC teachers: "I think most left [the institute] feeling somewhat fearful around how they would continue this work when they had 33 students in the classroom and just them. It will help if they have the

Parent Partner because now they will have a parent who went through the practicum and who understands a little bit about [student-centered] teaching and learning."[3]

COMMUNITY MEMBERS

Community members champion teachers' learning and community by becoming knowledgeable advocates for their efforts. However, this support is usually another missing link in teachers' professional context. School boards, for example, are "the forgotten players of the education team," and learning opportunities rarely are provided for them (Danzinger quoted in Fullan, 2001, p. 208). Admittedly, it is no easy matter for boards to learn as a team, since meetings are public and often political. Strategies effective in promoting board member knowledge are very intentional in providing opportunities for district trustees to learn about classroom-level efforts and the issues confronting administrators and teachers as they seek to improve student learning. One Bay Area district we studied for several years includes board members in districtwide strategic planning sessions that require examination of data, reviewing promising practices, and skilled facilitation. The board not only supports reform, but has been enthusiastic about enhancing their knowledge of the reform work. Some districts invite board members to attend conferences and workshops with central office staff or participate in district retreats.

Community members and school boards can learn about reforms and teachers' learning goals in a number of ways: through participating in such activities as workshops given by teachers, school districts, or educational organizations; by collaborating with teachers and students on class projects; and by volunteering in a classroom. Some cities have called "educational summits" in an effort to build a sense of communitywide identity and engagement with teachers' work and the civic capacity to support education. In this way, community members develop tacit understandings as well as explicit knowledge of curricular, assessment, or pedagogical reforms. By witnessing reform up close, community members are in a better position to understand the nuances, challenges, and values that underlie their district's reform undertakings and teachers' goals.

For example, in what a Chicago SATC art project director called a "purely political move," influential community members were invited to participate in the project's field trip and seminar. As a consequence, they became enthusiastic proponents of arts in the schools, and lobbied effectively for board support in the face of budget cuts. The Chicago SATC project also made art enthusiasts through their Spiritual Passports and Transformative Journeys Art Show, which featured the artwork and descriptive writing of students from across Chicago. Public response exceeded the hopes and expectations of participating teachers, students, and their collaborators. It provided a major boost not only for the arts, but for Chicago's much-maligned public schools. Those attending were struck by the quality of the students' work and the students' high level of engagement. Press coverage of the event provided a cheering counterpoint to a dispiriting season of media emphasis on student and school failure. Raymond Coffey of the *Chicago Sun-Times* (1998) wrote glowingly that the exhibit, involving 2,000 kids from a dozen city schools, was "remarkable, engaging, and high-quality." His closing paragraph points to the event as evidence of the exciting potential of the Chicago public school students: "The exhibit is intended mainly for the kids—an opportunity to meet and mix with their counterparts from other schools. It is not open to the general public. Too bad, in the future somehow it ought to be. It would give anyone worried about kids a big lift."

EXPANDING THE LOCAL LEARNING AGENDA

Society invests in teachers' learning and professional communities because it hopes to boost student achievement. But the nature of teachers' learning opportunities, and their classroom consequences, necessarily implicates the learning of a greater circle of actors, inside and outside district boundaries. High-quality teacher resources are necessary, but not enough, to establish the school and classroom practices that foster better student achievement. The sustainable, reflective classroom practices linked to student achievement occur when key actors in the district and community become knowledgeable about teachers' instructional activities and the educational goals they pursue and actively support them.

What does this learning entail? Administrators, parents, and community members benefit, just as teachers do, from opportunities that are interactive, hands-on, and situated in real issues and practices. Like teachers, these groups benefit when learning occasions are multiple, overlapping, and goal-focused, and when learning occurs in a collaborative environment that focuses on problem-solving and reflection. Designing and accomplishing such an expanded learning agenda is harder and less familiar than the challenge of providing helpful resources for individual teachers and schools. Providing intentional learning opportunities for the people in teachers' broader professional context requires very different conceptions of the "learning problem," what needs to change, how to bring that change about, and how to sustain it. And an expanded local learning agenda calls for the political will necessary to support it—both in spirit and in reality.

7

A Local Learning System to Support Teacher Learning Communities

School-based teacher learning communities can create the new knowledge and new norms of practice essential to answering society's call for more challenging instruction and equitable outcomes for America's diverse student body. Teachers—education's "street level bureaucrats," (Weatherley & Lipsky, 1977)—can transform more demanding standards for student learning into improved classroom practices only if they understand them and their significance for their students, and come to hold them as their own.

School-based teacher communities are both the site and source of learning—they generate and use knowledge in ways not possible in other settings because learning starts with particular goals for particular students. School-based communities of practice are essential to creating the norms of collective responsibility and continual learning required of the teaching profession. They form the core of a new professionalism because they afford opportunities for teachers to take responsibility for their own learning and that of their students.

WHY ARE TEACHER LEARNING COMMUNITIES RARE?

Despite compelling evidence of their special value to teaching and learning, school-based teacher learning communities are neither common in American schools nor featured as policy responses to improving student outcomes. Chapter 2 details the challenges implicit in the change in professional culture assumed by teacher learning communities. In addition to these normative constraints, many aspects of the education policy environment are uncongenial to their development and sustainability.

For one, building and sustaining teacher learning communities in schools involves more complex and demanding processes than many reformers want to consider in a "quick-fix" reform context. Also, reformers of the command-and-control stripe worry that investments in teacher learning communities are ill-placed because they consign responsibility for learning to the hands of those targeted to change, teachers. These reformers' investments instead concentrate on external knowledge resources to the exclusion of support for in-school learning and knowledge creation. The "problem" to be "fixed" in this approach features individual teachers, not their up-close professional context or community. Ironically, in this day of "evidence-based" decision-making and policy, research-based consensus on elements of effective professional development and theories of learning are all but ignored as investments are made in knowledge resources to improve teachers' instructional capability.

More important than neglect by reformers, though, are other features of the education policy context that are inhospitable or actively contrary to the development or prosperity of teacher learning communities in schools. Swings in the local education landscape matter to a learning community's stability. School-based teacher learning communities often fall apart in the face of local shifts in leadership and changing political tastes. Local leaders new to the district scene, especially superintendents, want to make a splashy impact. However, teacher learning communities are neither flashy nor sexy as a priority for district change compared to such high-visibility reform measures as new curriculum adoption. Building and sustaining high-functioning teacher learning communities in schools entails slow, steady effort.

Some prominent state and federal policies push against factors fundamental to developing and sustaining teacher learning communities. Set against the broader policy environment, the requirements of a strong teacher learning community represent a classic macro/micro mismatch between policy system tools, power dynamics, and resources at the top of the system and frames for action at the bottom, in schools and classrooms. District-, state-, and federal-level policymakers have different policy "keyboards" at their disposal, and they frequently operate according to contrary logics of change. For example, policymakers seek uniformity and coherence across systems. But when standards are treated as rigid rules rather than as guides for teaching and learning, teachers have little room to contribute their own knowledge and judgment as they develop practices intended to meet those standards. Similarly, high-stakes accountability systems feature narrow tests of student achievement that limit teachers' ability to learn about students' understanding and learning and too often restrict their focus to easily measurable outcomes. These systems create disincentives for teachers to take responsibility for their own continuing learning and students' outcomes, and perhaps foster competition among schools and teachers.

Likewise, norm-based accountability systems provide slim feedback to teachers about how to do better and are of little value to teacher learning communities. Instead, these policies create strong deterrents to teachers' engagement in the active examination of instructional alternatives of the kind that provide powerful building blocks for teachers' knowledge base and professional repertoire. Other policies aimed at improving schools can derail teacher communities. For instance, district reconstitution strategies that take apart and then reassemble a school's faculty as a response to unacceptable student outcomes in many instances destroy the resource best able to improve students' learning—the teachers' professional community (Mintrop, 2004). Likewise, district policies for teacher assignment or reassignment of teachers that ignore the character of community at the school level can capsize it (see Gamoran et al., 2003).

Local responses to state and federal mandates differ across districts and play out differently in terms of impact on teacher learning communities in schools. For example, in addition to testing requirements that can frustrate the inquiry efforts of teacher learning communities, the massive federal education act, No Child Left Behind (NCLB), requires evidence of "highly qualified teachers" at work in schools receiving federal dollars. This requirement prompts districts to scramble to put together credential-granting "high-quality professional development" to meet that mandate. Because federal Title I funds are a primary source of local professional development dollars, however, the NCLB's requirements likely will pull away teacher learning resources available at the school level to underwrite discrete district-level professional development activities and off-site degree-granting courses.

Teacher learning communities' resource requirements present practical obstacles. Learning communities in schools need material, human, and social resources that either do not exist in most settings, or are in short supply where they are found (see Gamoran et al., 2003). Learning communities require time and space, scarce resources in the context of overcrowded facilities and working days tightly scheduled and often constrained by union contracts.

Even where these immediate and practical issues are resolved, learning communities in schools need ongoing human resources, a coordinator or a coach—someone to nurture development, monitor teachers' progress and needs, assist with inquiry, and broker access to knowledge resources in the broader environment. Experience suggests that this need does not go away once a learning community is established. Facilitation, brokering, and convening are fundamental needs of a learning community that must be met consistently and in a timely way. And they must be someone's responsibility, rather than tacked onto the job of an already overloaded department chair, teacher leader, or administrator. The responsibility merits title, dedicated time, and line-item provision in school or district budgets.

Professional developers or externally based facilitators serving as critical friends, called by whatever name, comprise another learning community basic (and expense) that continues to matter even in mature groups. Professional developers bring expert assistance and best practices to the school; they provide critical feedback of the kind only a friendly outsider can. Yet the existing corps of professional developers falls far short of demand in most districts both in quality and quantity, and the policy environment operates in ways that compromise these essential resources. For one, professional developers' or coaches' learning needs are not considered a system concern, but are instead left up to these individuals or their organizations. Another fact of district life works against the quality and availability of these crucial learning resources: competitive bidding. School or district contracts typically are awarded to the lowest bidder, rather than to the professional developer with proven expertise and considered most suitable to address learning needs. Investment in strong professional developers ranks among the most highly leveraged outlays a district could make. The learning that occurs within schools and throughout the system can only be as good as the knowledge resources that support it; capacity-building requires capacity.

For all of these reasons—political will, the local reform agenda and responses to state and federal policies, district personnel and budget choices— questions about how to develop, nurture, and sustain teacher learning communities in schools implicate the system within which they operate. Understanding of how and what teachers need to learn comprises a bottom-line requirement of a policy context that supports school-based teacher learning communities.

THE DISTRICT AS THE UNIT OF CHANGE

The district is the system context of greatest significance for teachers' school-based learning communities. M. Bruce King (2004), Fred Newmann and Associates (1996), Adam Gamoran and colleagues (2003), James Spillane and Charles Thompson (1997), and others underscore the important role district leaders play in fostering and preserving strong professional communities at the school level, and stress that district leaders need to pay attention to how school faculty learn and develop together. We argue similarly that workforce development strategies grounded in teachers' learning require school and district level leadership. Though it is possible for a strong school-based learning community to develop despite the district, it is unlikely that it can be sustained or extended to other schools if the district is not actively supportive (Center for Research on the Context of Teaching, 2002).

Districts matter for the operation and effectiveness of school-based teacher learning communities in several ways. Leadership is essential, of course, and district indifference or shifts in priorities affect school-level choices and opportunities. Teacher learning communities within schools exist in a complex system environment of regulations, rules, resources, expectations, past investments, and political expectations. These factors have to be aligned and rationalized at the system level in service of coherence-making if teacher learning communities are to enjoy consistent messages about expectations for the classroom. Berends, Bodilly, and Kirby (2002), for example, highlight the ways in which incoherent district systems derailed school-level reform efforts sponsored by the New American Schools initiative (see also McLaughlin & Talbert, 2002, on the ways in which district policies and messages affect teachers and principals). System-level leadership is needed to link teacher learning to system priorities and reform initiatives.

Sustainable, rigorous teacher learning communities require district leaders who manage the bad news data can bring and model candor in discussing student outcomes and implications for practice at all levels of the system. Experience teaches that evidence of failure or shortfall can galvanize teachers' learning, and candor defines a strong learning community. However, in education it seems that "spin" or cover-up often are more attractive options than public display of disappointing outcomes. Strong leadership and unwavering endorsement of the need to consider areas for improvement as well as to celebrate success create teachers' sense of psychological and professional safety. The evidence necessary to inform decisions about instruction and resource allocation up and down the system necessarily speaks to the uneven performance of particular schools and student groups. Leaders must manage these hot-button issues with various constituencies—the school board, parents, the union—if school-based teacher communities are to persist and thrive.

On the topic of confronting failure, the organizational culture of schools and school districts stands in stark contrast to that of so-called high-performance organizations—team-based organizations such as nuclear power plants, hospitals, and aerospace that cannot afford failure. These organizations take evidence of failure as signal of needed improvements, rather than cause for blame. Debra Meyerson (personal communication, April 18, 2005) encountered a vivid example of celebration of mistakes on a Gulf of Mexico oil platform. To reinforce the importance of learning, the platform crew had established the "Million Dollar Club" in mocking reference to the corporate club of the same name. Unlike the corporate version established to recognize salespeople who sold one million dollars worth of products, however, employees on the platform who were initiated into the club had made an error that *cost* the company one million dollars. The club and the playful ritual that accompanied it legitimated talking about mistakes so that employees could learn from them, and served as a visible symbol of the company's commitment to learning from experience. Likewise, the medical community has organized rituals to review errors and learn from them. The Morbidity and Mortality Conference, which usually takes place once a week in academic hospitals across the country, provides a place where doctors can talk frankly with one another about their mistakes and consider what to do differently (Gawande, 2000). Few districts have such norms or venues for candid examination of shortfalls and opportunities to learn from experience.

Taking the district as the unit of change shifts thinking about schools as geographical constituencies or distinct organizational entities to a districtwide consideration of teaching and learning and assessment of strengths, problems, and opportunities. Taking the district as the unit of change also shifts thinking about educational improvement strategies from those trying to "improve" teachers to those intending to improve a system of supports for teachers' learning and community—a longer-term, capacity-building strategy. This perspective on teachers' learning needs indicates that while *extent* of district support for teachers' professional development makes a difference, it is *how* the resources are allocated that matters most to teachers' learning community. In particular, do resource allocation strategies signal a conception of the district as a learning system?

THE DISTRICT AS A LOCAL LEARNING SYSTEM

The vigor of a school-based learning community depends fundamentally on the norms, supports, and expectations in its broader environment and the presence of a local learning agenda that furthers teachers' school-based communities. Enacting that agenda requires infrastructure, coordination, production of data, and capacity for analysis as well as expectations of everyone for ongoing learning—in other words, a local learning system, not just a data management strategy. A local learning system deepens, sustains, and extends school-based teacher learning communities. It takes a broad focus for learning and ensures that all of a district's educators and administrators are exposed to high-quality learning opportunities, not only those individuals motivated to attend on their own, or required by special project guidelines to participate.

A learning system perspective holds the district responsible for meeting the diverse needs of the teacher workforce—and doing so in ways that reinforce and extend the work of school-based learning communities. This view includes all schools and teachers in district reform efforts, albeit in different ways and at different levels. It stands in contrast to the one-school-at-a-time approach to school reform that motivated prominent reform efforts such as Theodore Sizer's Coalition for Essential Schools, Robert Slavin's Success for All, James Comer's School Development Project, or the federal Comprehensive School Reform Demonstration program. A learning system perspective directs district attention to learning requirements across the system and calls for a menu of resources to meet the learning needs of individuals at different stages in their career, with different responsibilities or awareness about local reform activities. As decades of negative reviews of in-service offerings attest, "one-size-fits-all" professional development occasions are largely a waste of time and resources.

A whole-district strategy contrasts with the *nonsystem* of learning resources that exists in most districts and teachers' professional lives—the hodgepodge of workshops, pet projects, and in-service requirements attached to disparate categorical or special initiatives. A learning system promotes coherence and enables cost-efficient investment in learning because professional development resources can be coordinated, not wasted when site- and district-level learning needs fail to connect. It establishes a district culture of learning and provides mutually reinforcing opportunities for gaining and generating new knowledge at all levels of the system.

Several elements distinguish a local learning system from "business as usual" in most of America's districts: a comprehensive plan detailing expectations for teaching and learning, integrated learning resources, development of local knowledge resources, and a robust data and accountability system. Strong, committed district leadership makes it happen.

A Comprehensive Plan

A learning system has a plan that describes system goals for teaching and learning, allocation of resources, and accountability. An inclusive plan for a learning system connects district-level goals to explicit expectations for schools and classrooms and evidence about them. It incorporates the needs and contributions of all stakeholders in the system—parents, students, and community as well as educators.

Integrated Learning Resources

District administrators think about and allocate resources differently when these decisions are made with an eye to supporting strong, vital teacher learning communities. A learning system stance directs administrators to map the totality of district resources from public and private sources for professional development, and assess both their coherence and distribution, in order to manage categorical resources in ways that minimize overlap and inconsistency of message or direction. Key questions are, Who is getting what and when? How do these capacity-building resources relate to one another? How do they address identified system needs? Do they provide differentiated learning supports?

Creation of Local Knowledge and Capacity

A local learning system identifies and uses strong school-based teacher learning communities as resources for district learning by exploiting naturally occurring variation in practices and outcomes across schools. A district might invest in small experiments or planned variations across schools or in district clusters or learning communities as a way to inform the district learning community and situate practice in local contexts. This strategy generates local knowledge of the most powerful kind because it permits teachers to get at theoretical explanations and principles of practice: Why did similar pedagogical strategies turn out differently in different settings or for different students? A local learning system invests in resources for teachers' professional development and supports for learning communities as a core priority rather than on the more typical "as possible" basis.

A Robust Data and Accountability System

Timely, relevant, accessible, and usable data comprise the *sine qua non* of a district learning system. A system that provides a comprehensive account of students' progress toward expectations includes both formative and summative data generated on a regular basis. Formative assessment forms an integral part of the assessments and highlights areas for instructional focus and change. Summative measures indicate patterns of progress within and across schools by such student demographics as ethnicity, economic status, and language proficiency. A learning system has technology to deliver information in a timely, user-friendly manner; everyone from the area manager to the classroom teacher needs access to up-to-date information.

Similarly, a high-performing human resources system possesses information about teachers' professional backgrounds and classroom effectiveness and about principals' particular strengths. This information plays an essential role as decisions are made about teacher and administrator assignment. Equity concerns call attention to the distribution of expertise within the system and assume procedures for assigning teachers and principals to schools that take school challenges and needs into account as well as the character of the existing teacher learning community. A cluster of "lemons" (a term often used to designate the least effective teachers) or overrepresentation of novice teachers in a school precludes formation of a strong teacher learning community because the expertise necessary to mentor less experienced or accomplished teachers does not exist in the workplace setting—the baseline capacity for building a learning community is absent. Just as teachers need evidence about their students' progress and accomplishments, district administrators need evidence about teachers' and principals' learning needs in order to carry out this distributional function.

A comprehensive data system also includes information about students' experiences. "Ask the client," a taken-for-granted tactic in marketing, finds little analogue in school improvement efforts. Yet teachers and administrators have much to gain from students' perceptions of school. A learning system benefits from students' assessments of their schools as educational environments and their classrooms as opportunities for them to learn. Systemwide evidence about students' perceptions and experiences can make particular contributions to educators' deliberations about how to improve teaching and learning in the district. Across the country, some school districts have made effective use of school climate surveys to assess factors such as students' motivation and engagement, student–teacher relationships, perceptions of belonging and safety, teachers' instructional management, and views about opportunities for participation in school-sponsored activities.[1]

Skilled and Committed Leadership

Skilled and committed district leadership provides essential normative and political support for the investments and changes assumed by a local learning system and pulls all of these elements together. Managing organizational culture to support inquiry and learning entails modeling of an inquiry stance and creation of a data culture by system leaders and political leadership to protect the investments required by a learning system. As one district's technology director put it: "The technical part—that's fairly standard. The toughest piece is changing the culture of the way people do things " (quoted in Mieles & Foley, 2005, p. 28). Moving to a data-driven local learning system requires profound changes in teachers' (and principals') professional culture. Changes involve not only expectations that educators will use a variety of evidence to make decisions about practice, but more significantly, that practice will be "deprivatized," or moved into the public view of colleagues and the community (see for example Petrides & Nodine, 2005). Leadership to motivate and support this kind of cultural shift has been rare in American school districts, since a learning posture and the uncertainty associated with it can be perceived as out of line with the popular image of a confident, competent leader. Yet without this political and normative leadership, the candid, evidence-based reflection on practice essential to instructional change carries risks for both teachers and principals. The relative scarcity of this kind of district leadership, more than inadequate technology or knowledge resources, impedes the development of comprehensive, integrated, fully functioning district learning systems.

IMPLEMENTING A LOCAL LEARNING AGENDA:
BOSTON PUBLIC SCHOOLS

Despite the difficult challenges entailed in developing and implementing a district learning system, especially in the country's large urban districts, some promising examples do exist and provide concrete illustration of what a district learning system looks like in practice. The Boston Public

Schools (BPS) provide perhaps the best-developed example of a district learning agenda grounded in teachers' collaborative, school-based learning, and data about outcomes for both students and adults in the district. Boston's local learning agenda incorporates to a greater or lesser extent all of the elements essential to a vital local learning system and therefore to productive school-based teacher learning communities.

A Comprehensive Plan

Boston's Whole-School Improvement strategy, a system-level plan that addresses all levels and actors in the district, puts data and evidence about student work at the center of improved classroom instruction and features school teams focused on planning students' instruction and addressing their own professional learning needs. It is based in a "workshop" instructional approach that takes students where they are, working intensely with them and frequently updating their learning goals. Boston's plan is organized around the "Six Essentials," which provide a framework and detail expectations for the work:

Effective Instruction (the core essential)
Student Work and Data
Professional Development
Shared Leadership
Resources
Families and Community

A wall chart elaborates the Six Essentials, the expectations they set, and the evidence expected to be seen when they are met. Its placement in schools and district offices serves as a visible symbol of the district's commitment to whole-school improvement.

Boston's Whole-School Improvement plan takes a broad view of "district" and stakeholders; parents and the community feature prominently. One of the "Six Essentials," parents and community members have been brought into the reform agenda and provided with learning resources. Based on the results of a Family and Community Engagement Task Force, the district appointed a Deputy Superintendent for Parent and Community Engagement and established an Office of Family and Community Engagement. This office actively reaches out to involve families, provides materials to deepen parents' knowledge about good instruction, and affords them support for working with their children at home. For example, the district made two videos for parents about reading aloud to their children. The local education fund, the Boston Plan for Excellence, involves leading citizens through its various boards and task forces. Most recently, civic leaders participated in a Principal for a Day program, an effort that brought many into direct and extended contact with Boston's schools for the first time.

Integrated Learning Resources

Professional development for Boston teachers takes place at the school and features a coaching strategy involving collaborative teacher groups. The district's Collaborative Coaching and Learning model (CCL), which provides intensive, ongoing professional development that fosters a more collaborative teacher culture, became district policy for all schools in 2003 and reflects the district's learning about how to foster learning for both teachers and students. Superintendent Thomas Payzant (n.d.) wrote in a letter to the community: "We have evidence from our own schools that when teachers learn together, students learn more."

CCL conceives of teachers' learning in the same way as the district's workshop approach to instruction understands students' learning—constructed through active participation. Elements of CCL include inquiry into practice and student learning and involve participating teachers in an 8-week cycle of organized professional talk. As part of a team, teachers study a strategy from Readers' or Writers' Workshops, observe colleagues' classrooms, and conduct demonstration lessons. The classroom serves as a laboratory for learning based in reflection, feedback, and inquiry. Participation is mandatory; every teacher must participate in a cycle. CCL uses collaboration among teachers as a way to transfer responsibility for professional development from a consultant-coach to school staff and to foster internal accountability for student learning. CCL's experiences show how schools can "grow" their own human resources and provide the needed room for teachers to try out new ideas, fail, and rethink practices (Guiney, 2005). Boston provides a separate professional development budget at every school with the goal of bringing learning resources as close to the school as possible. In this way, school-level professional development is both job-embedded and explicitly connected to the district's goals.

Creating Local Knowledge and Capacity

Boston's strategy attends explicitly to the creation of new knowledge within the system and features learning from variation and pilots of promising practices in district schools. The district's Effective Practices (EP) policy identifies schools to test out ideas that push school improvement. This R&D strategy, with its explicit embrace of "trials" carried out in the network of EP schools, generates local knowledge and concrete capacity to further whole-school improvement across the district. The EP schools provide "social proof" of the value of an inquiry culture and critical examination of alternatives to existing practices.

As a result of the EP work, in 2003 superintendent Thomas Payzant allocated resources to provide significant supports for coaches' own learning and professional development. Payzant's decision, made in tight fiscal times, recognized the progress associated with intensive coaching in EP schools; the demonstrated limitations of the district's previous, less-intensive coaching model; and the imperative to invest in coaches' own learning if they are to function most effectively. As a result, Boston's coaches have a level of professional development resources beyond those found in most other districts. All school coaches participate in a 3-day training institute every August and attend a 7-hour professional development session every other Friday throughout the school year.

Data Systems

The Boston Plan for Excellence (BPE), the community's local education fund, developed a "data warehouse," the FAST Track system, to help schools manage the multiple sources and types of data schools need to inform instruction and professional development. FAST Track allows schools to combine student demographic data from the district's report-generating systems, schools' local assessments, and student performance data on high-stakes assessments such as the Massachusetts Comprehensive Assessment (MCAS) and the Stanford 9 into a single interface. The district replicated many FAST Track functions it its design of the MyBPS system, a districtwide portal that provides information to all members of the BPS community and is updated every evening. MyBPS acknowledges that data needs differ at different levels of the system and so includes data relevant to the work of central office staff as well as teachers' classrooms. The Boston Plan for Excellence provides key supports for teachers' data use. BPE developed FAST-R (Formative Assessment of Student Thinking in Reading), a series of short, low-stakes formative assessments based on reading passages from the MCAS exams, and provides on-site support to use the tools. BPE hires and funds skilled former teachers to serve as site-based implementation coaches. BPS returns the test results within a week; coaches help teachers consider their practices in light of the results and work with the school's literacy coach and principal to integrate data into the school's ongoing professional development.

Skilled and Committed Leadership

Managing the transformation from one set of professional beliefs or from one organizational culture to another presents a critical task for leadership, but one often ignored or put aside in the press of district business. The Boston superintendent's commitment to using data and learning through collaborative inquiry has been explicit and unwavering. For example, in a letter to district educators, Payzant (n.d.) acknowledged how difficult it might be for many teachers to give a demonstration lesson for their colleagues and underscored the importance of this collaborative learning strategy, as supported by the district's own research. Although Boston experienced significant fiscal stress, Payzant gave steadfast support to especially vulnerable elements of the strategy that he believed essential to a successful learning system—coaches in every school, professional development for them, and substantial outreach to parents and community. Expenditures of this sort typically have been hard to defend when budget balancers pledge to keep cuts "as far from the classroom as possible." Despite complaints from the teacher union, Payzant made and defended these hard choices in the belief that well-prepared school coaches and knowledgeable parents and community were integral, not incidental, to teachers' classroom effectiveness and the success of the district's Whole-School Improvement strategy.

OUTCOMES OF BOSTON'S LEARNING SYSTEM

Multiple evaluations show that Boston's approaches to instruction—the workshop model—and to professional development—Collaborative Coaching and Learning (CCL)—are benefiting students and teachers. Student outcomes have improved, as have relationships between teachers and students and among teachers (Boston Plan for Excellence and the Boston Public Schools, 2004). Boston sees other positive system-level consequences of their strategy—enhanced coherence, increased accountability at all levels, and increased buy-in from district educators.

Tight–Loose Coupling

School districts' famously "loosely coupled" nature (Weick, 1976) challenges the system to learn from and about activities taking place in small groups such as the school-based teacher teams or schools themselves. The Boston learning system's multiple strategies of integration within and across the district go a long way to ensure consistency and coherence. The district Wall Chart of Six Essentials sets out explicit expectations for both schools and central administrators for each element. Inclusion of central office administrators signals Payzant's commitment to reciprocal accountability and defines clear evidence of "What you should see and hear . . . " if essentials are being addressed in the classroom, school, and central office. Boston provides professional development for district administrators so they understand what to look for in the schools and what supports they are to provide. BPS also acted to dissolve the bifurcation between district instructional and human resources staff. The district has focused on the critical role of its human resources department and acted to bring it into the reform and develop teacher hiring and retention policies that support the whole-school improvement agenda.

Boston's experience sheds light on how to manage the tension between supporting teachers' professional autonomy and at the same time bringing coherence to the system. Through CCL, teachers' learning links to the larger system and adds up to an articulated resource for school improvement across the district. Further, the superintendent regularly convenes a teacher advisory group to elicit school-level feedback on how district reform strategies are working or not. These district-level learning resources and expectations recognize the interdependence of teacher and organizational learning—that the district as an organization cannot learn if its members do not learn. And, conversely, if the central office does not learn, it is difficult for teachers to act on their new knowledge and understanding or sustain and deepen their knowledge base. In contrast to the Boston example, disconnections between many BASRC schools and their districts illustrate how energetic and enthusiastic inquiry-based learning at the school level was dampened and limited in its influence on the broader school system because opportunities or motivation for learning were absent at the central office level. Pockets of impressive school-level learning had no larger impact on the system when they went unobserved by the central office. Boston's investments in system learning are expressly intended to connect learning and change throughout the system through "tight–loose" coupling.

Reciprocal Accountability

Students of complex system reform maintain that a combination of administrative and professional accountability comprises the essential foundation of lasting reform (see O'Day, 2002). Anthony Alvarado (1998) calls this "reciprocal accountability" and asserts that it is a *system failure*, not an individual failure, when those supports are lacking and student outcomes fall short. Reciprocal accountability comes alive in the BPS wall chart. The system itself is accountable to teachers and principals for providing the resources and assistance they need to meet expectations. The wall chart establishes expectations and evidence of performance for administrators and educators in the system. The FAST Track data warehouse and MyBPS provide information on both student achievement and adult accomplishments. District administrators' evaluations highlight the extent to which they have functioned as useful resources for schools; principals' assessments comment on the extent to which they have supported teacher inquiry, collaboration, and instructional improvement; teachers' evaluations note student learning outcomes as well as their involvement in professional development activities and the school-level learning community. The result is heightened mutual accountability in teacher learning communities throughout the system.

Creating a Social Movement

Boston's experience points out that a learning system in which everyone participates can provide the environment of a social movement. Teachers and principals in Boston comment that they feel they are part of something important, a reform undertaking bigger than the school and larger than themselves (Boston Plan for Excellence and the Boston Public Schools, 2004). They feel energized by the sense that what they do matters to more than their classroom or school. In this way, a learning system can capture momentum built on the ground as a system resource.

RESEARCH FOR SCHOOL-BASED LEARNING COMMUNITIES

Research focused on school-based learning communities can play an important role in fostering a supportive context for their creation and support. Little existing research directly examines institution-building *within* organizations, and the evolution and contribution of teacher learning communities within schools provide no exception. The absence of policy support for school-based learning communities in part reflects the lack of systematic information about them as a learning resource for teachers. Available evidence about the relationship between school-based teacher learning communities and positive student outcomes is promising and consistent—but thin. Evaluative research that documents the role of school-based teacher learning communities and consequences for students would inform a theory of *changing* and contribute important new evidence to the policy community at all levels.

A considerable body of theoretical and empirical literature exists about the design principles associated with communities of practice and effective learning environments. We know quite a bit about the structures, relationships, and activities associated with effective professional development efforts. We know much less about the process—*how* teacher learning communities get started, how they develop, and how requirements for their development and markers of maturity change. This book provides illustrations of these trajectories, but much more is needed. Documentation and analysis of teacher learning communities in diverse settings and at different points in their evolution would provide a cornerstone for local learning systems.

Notes

Chapter 1

1. NELS: 88 is a federal research program that follows a national sample of students who were 8th graders in 1988 through their education and into the workforce. It surveyed students and teachers and tested students every 2 years, yielding student data for 8th, 10th, and 12th grades and beyond.

2. This analysis used a school survey measure of "inquiry practices" and estimated its effect on 2001 SAT-9 scores after 1998 SAT-9 scores were controlled. Results were consistent for two samples of BASRC schools: 18 schools for which mean teacher survey ratings were analyzed and 52 schools for which a reform coordinator's ratings were used. For details, see Center for Research on the Context of Teaching (2002). These evaluations and the instruments they employed are available at: http://www.stanford.edu/group/CRC/.

Chapter 4

1. As further information: the practicum was held at a selected school site in each cluster, was offered two to three times each of two summers, and involved teams of four teachers and two parents from each school. Students who participated in practicum classes were from grades 3–7 and grades 9–11.

Chapter 5

1. This report and case studies may be downloaded free of charge from www.learningfirst.org. Case study districts included Aldine Independent School District, TX; Chula Vista Elementary School District, CA; Kent County Public Schools, MD; Minneapolis Public Schools, MN; and Providence Public Schools, RI.

2. The six Standards of Effective Instruction included in the union contract explicate what and how teachers are expected to learn:

1. Teachers are committed to students and their learning.
2. Teachers have a depth of knowledge of the subjects they teach and how to teach those subjects to students.
3. Teachers manage and monitor student learning for continuous improvement and progress.
4. Teachers reflect systematically about their practice and learn from experience.
5. Teachers participate as members of learning communities.
6. Teachers commit to professional development consistent with Minnesota Basic and High Standards, National Standards, and alignment of standards and goals. (Togneri & Anderson, 2003, p. 16)

Chapter 6

1. BASRC's "executive coach" strategy provides an exception to this general statement. BASRC teams up executive coaches, who are former superintendents, with superintendents in the initiative's "focal districts." They work together with district leaders to implement districtwide reform. It is too early to assess the consequences of this work for superintendents' knowledge and leadership skills, but early evidence paints a mixed picture of the "fit" between coach and the receptivity of the superintendent to be coached (see Coggins, 2005).

2. Jim Vopat, creator of the Parent Project, is a professor at Carroll College, a Fulbright scholar, and director of the Milwaukee Writing Project. His 1994 book, *The Parent Project: A Workshop Approach to Parent Involvement*, brought the insights of reading/writing workshops and inquiry learning to parent education efforts. His latest book (with contributions by Pete Leki), *More Than Bake Sales: The Resource Guide for Family Involvement in Education* (1998), shows step by step how schools can create parent involvement programs that transcend shallow volunteerism, and grow deep, substantive partnerships. Vopat's parent involvement model was recognized by the Clinton administration as one of the most promising educational innovations in the country, and has been replicated in many schools throughout Chicago.

3. Parents also learned skills that led a number of them to enroll in GED, continuing education, or other education programs, and to find jobs. Through the institutes and their subsequent work as Parent Partners, parents learned how to use technology, and they also learned new ways of working with a range of people—community members, school visitors, district administrators, researchers. Parents' writing skills improved through the institute's practice of keeping

journals and through their classroom work with children. For example, a parent who took a computer course at the Beaver College Institute and became a Parent Partner subsequently enrolled at Beaver with the goal of becoming an elementary schoolteacher. A parent who had dropped out of high school to have her child credits the project for motivating her to get her GED and for the new self-esteem she acquired. "I had always been a nobody. Just a mother. Now [considering possibilities in front of me] I feel like Alice in Wonderland."

Chapter 7

1. The NASSP School Climate Survey reports a relationship between students' perceptions of school climate and academic achievement. For example, The 2003 National School Climate Survey sponsored by the Gay, Lesbian and Straight Education Network (2004) reports a direct relationship between school victimization in school, academic achievement, and educational aspirations of lesbian, gay, bisexual, and transgender (LGBT) students. LGBT youth who report significant and unrestrained verbal harassment are twice as likely to say that they do not intend to go to college, and their GPAs are significantly lower. Students who knew of no policy in place to protect them were 40% more likely to skip school (available online).

References

Achinstein, B. (2002). *Community, diversity, and conflict among schoolteachers: The ties that blind.* New York: Teachers College Press.

Alvarado, A. (1998, Winter). Professional development *is* the job. *American Educator,* pp. 18-23.

American Federation of Teachers. (1999, August 19). Redesigning low-performing schools: It's union work. http://www.aft.org/pubs-reports/downloads/teachers/redlps.pdf. Downloaded 8/29/03.

Argyris, C. (1982). *Reasoning, learning, and action.* San Francisco: Jossey-Bass.

Barth, R. S. (2001). *Learning by heart.* San Francisco: Jossey-Bass.

Bascia, N. (2003). Triage or tapestry? Teacher Unions' work toward improving teacher quality in an era of systemic reform. Seattle: University of Washington, Center for the Study of Teaching and Policy.

Berends, M., Bodilly, S., & Kirby, S. N. (2002). *Facing the challenges of whole-school reform.* Santa Monica, CA: The RAND Corporation.

Boston Plan for Excellence & the Boston Public Schools. (2004). *Whole-school improvement in Boston: Report to the Annenberg Foundation. School Year 2003–2004.* Boston: Author.

Bransford, J. D., Brown, A. L., & Cocking, R. R. (Eds). (1999). *How people learn: Brain, mind, experience, and school.* Washington, DC: National Academy Press.

Brouillette, L. (1996). *A geology of school reform: The successive restructuring of a school district.* Albany: State University of New York Press.

Brown, J. S., & Duguid, P. (2000). *The social life of information.* Cambridge, MA: Harvard Business School Press.

Burch, P. E. (2000). *Moving from the margins to the mainstream: Teaching and learning reform in local policy context.* Unpublished doctoral dissertation, Stanford University, Stanford, CA.

Carini, P. (1993). *The descriptive review of the child: A revision.* North Bennington, VT: Prospect Center.

Center for Research on the Context of Teaching, Stanford University. (1999). *Students at the center: Year three.* Stanford, CA: Author.

Center for Research on the Context of Teaching, Stanford University. (2002). *Bay Area School Reform Collaborative: Phase one (1996–2001) evaluation.* Stanford, CA: Author.

Center for the Study of Teaching and Policy, University of Washington. (n.d.). Unpublished field notes. Seattle, WA: Author.

Cochran-Smith, M., & Lytle, S. L. (1999). Relationships of knowledge and practice: Teacher learning in communities. *Review of Research in Education, 24*(2), 249–305.

Coffey, R. (1998, June 4). Student exhibit inspires hope and pride. *Chicago Sun Times.*

Coggins, C. T. (2005). *Coaching as a districtwide reform strategy.* Unpublished doctoral dissertation, Stanford University, Stanford, CA.

Cohen, D. K., & Hill, H. C. (2001). *Learning policy: When state education works.* New Haven, CT: Yale University Press.

Donovan, M. S., & Bransford, J. D. (Eds.). (2005). *How students learn: History, mathematics and science in the classroom.* Washington, DC: National Academy Press.

Eilers, A., Vagle, N., & Talbert, J. (2004, August). *High school professional communities: The case of a cross-discipline SLC team.* Paper presented at a TERC conference, "Supporting Professional Communities through Technology."

Finley, M. K. (1984). Teachers and tracking in a comprehensive high school. *Sociology of Education, 57,* 233–243.

Freeman, D. (1999). *Towards a descriptive theory of teacher learning and change.* Brattleboro, VT: Center for Teacher Education, Training and Research, School for International Training.

Friedrich, L. D. (2001). *Generating knowledge for practice: Joint work among teacher professional development organizations.* Unpublished doctoral dissertation, Stanford University, Stanford, CA.

Fullan, M. (2001). *The new meaning of education change* (3rd ed.). New York: Teachers College Press.

Gamoran, A., Anderson, C. W., Quiroz, P. A., Secada, W. G., Williams, T., & Ashmann, S. (2003). *Transforming teaching in math and science: How schools and districts can support change.* New York: Teachers College Press.

Gawande, A. (2000). When doctors make mistakes. In J. Gleick (Ed.), *The best American science writing 2000* (pp. 1–22). New York: Ecco Press.

Gay, Lesbian and Straight Education Network. (2004). The 2003 National School Climate Survey. Available online at www.glsen.org

Gutierrez, R. (1996). Practices, beliefs and cultures of high school math departments: Understanding their influence on student learning. *Journal of Curriculum Studies, 28,* 495–529.

Hargreaves, A. (1991). Contrived collegiality: The micro-politics of teacher collaboration. In J. Blaise (Ed.), *The politics of life in schools* (pp. 46–72). New York: Sage.

Hawley, W. D., & Valli, L. (1999). The essentials of effective professional development: A new consensus. In L. Darling-Hammond & G. Sykes (Eds.), *Teaching as a learning profession: Handbook of policy and practice* (pp. 127–150). San Francisco: Jossey-Bass.

Henderson, A. T., & Mapp, K. L. (2002). *A new wave of evidence: The impact of family, school and community connections on student achievement.* Austin, TX: National Center for Family and Community Connections with Schools, Southwest Educational Development Laboratory.

Hightower, A. M., Knapp, M. S., Marsh, J. A., & McLaughlin, M. W. (2002). *School districts and instructional renewal: Opening the conversation.* New York: Teachers College Press.

Hill, P. T., Campbell, C., & Harvey, J. (2000). *It takes a city: Getting serious about urban school reform.* Washington, DC: Brookings.

Ingram, D., Louis, K. S., & Schroeder, R. (June, 2004). Accountability policies and teacher decision making: Barriers to the use of data to improve practice. *Teachers College Record, 106(6),* 1258–1287.

King, M. B. (2004). School- and district-level leadership for teacher workforce development: Enhancing teacher learning and capacity. In M. A. Smylie & D. Miretzky (Eds.), *Developing the teacher workforce* (103rd Yearbook of the National Society for the Study of Education. Part 1). Chicago: University of Chicago Press.

Knapp, M. (1999). President's November newsletter. Available online at http: www.sdea.net. Downloaded November 30, 1999.

Koppich, J. E., & Kerchner, C. E. (1999). Organizing the other half of teaching. In L. Darling-Hammond & G. Sykes (Eds.), *Teaching as the learning profession* (pp. 315–341). San Francisco: Jossey-Bass.

Lee, V. E., & Smith, J. B. (1995). Effects of high school restructuring and size on gains in achievement and engagement for early secondary school students. *Sociology of Education, 68,* 241–270.

Lee, V. E., & Smith, J. B. (1996). Collective responsibility for learning and its effects on gains in achievement for early secondary school students. *American Journal of Education, 104,* 103–147.

Lee, V. E., Smith, J. B., & Croninger, R. G. (1997). How high school organization influences the equitable distribution of learning in mathematics and science. *Sociology of Education, 70,* 128–150.

Levitt, B., & March, J. G. (1988). Organizational learning. *Annual Review of Sociology, 114,* 319–340.

Lieberman, A., & Wood, D. R. (2003). *Inside the National Writing Project: Connecting network learning and classroom teaching.* New York: Teachers College Press.

Little, J. W. (1982). Norms of collegiality and experimentation: Workplace conditions of school success. *American Educational Research Journal, 19,* 325–340.

Lortie, D. C. (1975). *Schoolteacher: A sociological study.* Chicago: University of Chicago Press.

Louis, K. S., & Marks, H. M. (1998, August). Does professional community affect the classroom? Teachers' work and student experiences in restructuring schools. *American Journal of Education, 106,* 532–575.

MacDonald, J. P., Mohr, N., Dichter, A., & McDonald, E. C. (2003). *The power of protocols: An educator's guide to better practice.* New York: Teachers College Press.

March, J. G. (1991). Exploration and exploitation in organizational learning. *Organizational Science, 2*(1), 71–87.

McLaughlin, M. W., & Mitra, D. (2003). *The cycle of inquiry as engine of school reform: Lessons from the Bay Area School Reform Collaborative.* Stanford, CA: Center for Research on the Context of Teaching, Sanford University.

McLaughlin, M. W., & Talbert, J. E. (2001). *Professional communities and the work of high school teaching.* Chicago: University of Chicago Press.

McLaughlin, M., & Talbert, J. E. (2002). *Reforming districts: How districts support school reform.* Seattle: Center for the Study of Teaching and Policy, University of Washington.

Mieles, T., & Foley, E. (2005). *From data to decisions: Lessons from school districts using data warehousing.* Providence, RI: Annenberg Institute for School Reform at Brown University.

Mintrop, H. (2004). *Schools on probation: How accountability works (and doesn't work).* New York: Teachers College Press.

Mohr, N., & Dichter, A. (2001). *Stages of team development: Lessons from the struggles of site-based management.* Providence, RI: Annenberg Institute for School Reform at Brown University.

National Association of Secondary School Principals. (2004). *Executive summary. Breaking ranks II: Strategies for leading high school reform.* Reston, VA: Author.

Newmann, F., & Associates. (1996). *Authentic achievement: Restructuring schools for intellectual quality.* San Francisco: Jossey-Bass.

O'Day, J. A. (2002). Complexity, accountability, and school improvement. *Harvard Educational Review, 72,* 293–329.

Page, R. N. (1991). *Lower-track classrooms: A curricular and cultural perspective.* New York: Teachers College Press.

Payzant, T. (n.d.). *CCL in tough times: Strategies to keep the work going.* Boston: Boston Plan for Excellence & Boston Public Schools.

Petrides, L., & Nodine, T. (2005, April). *Anatomy of school system improvement: Performance-driven practices in urban school districts.* Half Moon Bay, CA: Institute for the Study of Knowledge Management of Education.

Putnam, R., & Borko, H. (2000). What do new views of knowledge and thinking have to say about research on teaching? *Educational Researcher, 29,* 4–15.

Richard, A. (2003). *The emergence of school-based staff developers in America's public schools.* Edna McConnell Clark Foundation. www.emcf.org/programs/student/student_pub.htm

Rowan, B., Chiang, F.-S., & Miller, R. J. (1997). Using research on employees' performance to study the effects of teachers on students' achievement. *Sociology of Education, 70,* 256–284

Sexton, R. F. (2004) *Mobilizing citizens for better schools.* New York: Teachers College Press.

Schön, D. (1983). *The reflective practitioner.* New York: Basic Books.

Simons, H., Kushner, S., & James, D. (2003, December). From evidence-based practice to practice-based evidence: The idea of situated generalization. *Research Papers in Education Policy and Practice, 18*(4), 347– 364.

Smylie, M. (1994). Redesigning teachers' work: Connections to the classroom. In L. Darling-Hammond (Ed.), *Review of Research in Education, 20,* (pp. 129–177). Washington, DC: American Education Research Association.

Spillane, J. P., & Thompson, C. I. (1997). Reconstructing conceptions of local capacity: The Local Education Agency's capacity for ambitious instructional reform. *Education Evaluation and Policy Analysis, 19*(2), 185–203.

Stein, M. K., Silver, E. A., & Smith, M. S. (1998). Mathematics reform and teacher development: A community of practice perspective. In J. G. Greeno & S. V. Goldman (Eds.), *Thinking practices in mathematics and science learning* (pp. 17–52). Mahwah, NJ: Erlbaum.

Stein, M. K., Smith, M. S., & Silver, E. A. (1999). The development of professional developers: Learning to assist teachers in new settings in new ways. *Harvard Educational Review. 69*(3), 237–269.

Stone, C., Henig, J., Jones, B. D., & Pierannunzi, C. (2001). *Building civic capacity: The politics of reforming urban schools.* Lawrence: University Press of Kansas.

Talbert, J. E., with Ennis, M. (1990). *Teacher tracking: Exacerbating inequalities in the high school.* Stanford, CA: Center for Research on the Context of Teaching, Stanford University.

Togneri, W., & Anderson, S. E. (2003). *Beyond islands of excellence: What districts can do to improve instruction and achievement in all schools.* Washington, DC: Learning First Alliance.

Tyack, D. B., & Cuban, L. (1996). *Tinkering toward utopia.* Cambridge, MA: Harvard University Press.

Vopat, J. (1994). *The parent project: A workshop approach to parent involvement.* Portland, ME: Stenhouse.

Vopat, J., & Leki, P. (1998). *More than bake sales: The resource guide for family involvement in education.* Portland, ME: Stenhouse.

Weatherley, R., & Lipsky, M. (1977, May). Street level bureaucrats and institutional information: Implementing special education reform. *Harvard Educational Review,* 21–28.

Weick, K. (1976). Educational organizations as loosely coupled systems. *Administrative Science Quarterly, 21*(1), 1–19.

Weick, K. E., Sutcliffe, K. M., & Obstfeld, D. (1999). Organizing for high reliability: Processes of collective mindfulness. *Research in Organizational Behavior, 21*, 81–123.

Wenger, E. (1998). *Communities of practice: Learning, meaning, and identity.* Cambridge, UK: Cambridge University Press.

Wenger, E., McDermott, R., & Snyder, W. M. (2003). *Cultivating communities of practice.* Cambridge, MA: Harvard Business School Press.

Yasumoto, J. Y., Uekawa. K., & Bidwell, C. E. (2001). The collegial focus and high school students' achievement. *Sociology of Education, 74*, 181–209.

Young, V. M. (2004). *Data-driven instruction: A view from the bottom up.* Paper presented at the Annual Meeting of the American Education Research Association, Montreal, Canada.

Index

About the Authors

Milbrey W. McLaughlin is the David Jacks Professor of Education and Public Policy at Stanford University. Professor McLaughlin is Co-director of the Center for Research on the Context of Teaching (CRC), founded in 1987. McLaughlin also is Executive Director of the John W. Gardner Center for Youth and Their Communities, a partnership between Stanford University and Bay Area communities. She is the author or coauthor of books on education policy issues, including *School Districts and Instructional Renewal* (with Amy Hightower, Michael Knapp, and Julie Marsh), 2002; *Communities of Practice and the Work of High School Teaching* (with Joan Talbert), 2001; *Community Counts: How Youth Organizations Matter for Youth Development*, 2000; *Teacher Learning: New Policies, New Practices* (with Ida Oberman), 1996; *Urban Sanctuaries: Neighborhood Organizations in the Lives and Futures of Inner-city Youth* (with Merita A. Irby and Juliet Langman), 2001; *Identity and Inner-city Youth: Beyond Ethnicity and Gender* (with Shirley Brice Heath), 1993; *Teaching for Understanding: Challenges for Policy and Practice* (with David K. Cohen and Joan E. Talbert), 1993; and *Teachers' Work* (with Judith Warren Little), 1993.

Joan E. Talbert is Senior Research Scholar and Co-director of the Center for Research on the Context of Teaching in the Stanford University School of Education. She received her B.A. from Vassar College, and M.A. and Ph.D. in Sociology from the University of Washington. Her books include *Professional Communities and the Work of High School Teaching* (with Milbrey W. McLaughlin), 2001; and *The Contexts of Teaching in Secondary Schools* (with Milbrey W. McLaughlin and Nina Bascia), 1990. Recent articles and book chapters include "Professionalism and Politics in High School Teaching Reform" (*Journal of Educational Change*), 2003; and "Reforming Districts" (in A. M. Hightower, M. S. Knapp, J. P. Marsh, and M. W. McLaughlin, Eds., *School Districts and Instructional Renewal: Opening the Conversation*), 2002.